sweet maple

ALSO FROM LYONS PRESS:

See page 28 for Michelle's Maple Sandwich Bread recipe.

sweet maple

BACKYARD SUGARMAKING FROM TAP TO TABLE

Michelle Visser

Foreword by Joel Salatin

LYONS
PRESS

GUILFORD, CONNECTICUT

An imprint of The Rowman & Littlefield Publishing Group, Inc.
4501 Forbes Blvd., Ste. 200
Lanham, MD 20706
www.rowman.com

Distributed by NATIONAL BOOK NETWORK

Copyright © 2019 by Michelle Visser

Jill's Maple BBQ Sauce recipe from *The Prairie Homestead Cookbook: Simple Recipes for Heritage Cooking in Any Kitchen* © 2019 by Jill Winger. Reprinted by Permission from Flatiron Books. All Rights Reserved.

All photographs by Michelle Visser except the following:

Popcorn photo on cover and photos on pages xii, 7, 9, 12, 48, 56, 59, 64, 81, and 153 by Hayley Visser.

Photo on opposite page by Jordyn Visser.

Photos on pages 62, 128, 168, and 190 by Kayla Visser.

Photos on page 25 by Jim Buetow, page 67 by Lou Plante, page 117 by Lindsey Baris, page 144 by Eric Hill, and page 197 by Abigail Lambert.

Photo of filtering on page 97 by Bryan Smagacz.

Photos on page 131 © LisaChristianson/iStock/Getty Images; page 133 (black maple) © SergeyTikhomirov/iStock/Getty Images; page 133 (red maple) © ClubhouseArts/iStock/Getty Images; page 134 (silver maple) and page 135 © seven75/iStock/Getty Images; page 134 (Norway maple) © Татьяна Санина/iStock/Getty Images; page 136 © Andrei Stanescu/iStock/Getty Images; page 137 © CampPhoto/iStock/Getty Images; page 138 (Rocky Mountain maple) © Eivaisla/iStock/Getty Images; page 138 (sycamore maple) © aaprophoto/iStock/Getty Images Plus; page 139 © ginton/iStock/Getty Images; page 140 (black walnut) © majorosl/iStock/Getty Images; page 140 (heartnut) © weisschr/iStock/Getty Images; page 140 (English walnut) © deyanarobova/iStock/Getty Images; page 141 © skhoward/iStock/Getty Images; page 142 (yellow birch) © ginton/iStock/Getty Images; page 142 (black birch) © Svtist/iStock/Getty Images; page 142 (river birch) © Joe_Potato/iStock/Getty Images; page 143 (gray birch) © ErikAgar/iStock/Getty Images; page 143 (European white birch) © Martin Wahlborg/iStock/Getty Images; page 143 (Alaskan white birch) © Pi-Lens/iStock/Getty Images; page 145 © ablokhin/iStock/Getty Images; page 146 (sweetgum) © Martina Simonazzi/iStock/Getty Images; page 146 (palm) © kendoNice/iStock/Getty Images; page 147 (shagbark hickory) © Westhoff/iStock/Getty Images; page 147 (tulip poplar) © OlyaSolodenko/iStock/Getty Images; page 148 © SandraMatic/iStock/Getty Images Plus

Photo on page 218 by Ayden Carpenter

Drawings on pages 20–21 by Jen Pries. IG: Jenny_Pries_Art

British Library Cataloguing in Publication Information available

Library of Congress Cataloging-in-Publication Data

Name: Visser, Michelle, author.
Title: Sweet maple : backyard sugarmaking from tap to table / Michelle Visser ; foreword by Joel Salatin.
Description: Guilford, Connecticut : Lyons Press, [2019] | Includes bibliographical references and index.
Identifiers: LCCN 2019018007 (print) | LCCN 2019018255 (ebook) | ISBN 9781493037780 (ebook)
  | ISBN 9781493037773 (pbk.)
Subjects: LCSH: Maple syrup.
Classification: LCC TP395 (ebook) | LCC TP395 .V58 2019 (print) | DDC 664/.132—dc23
LC record available at https://lccn.loc.gov/2019018007

♾️™ The paper used in this publication meets the minimum requirements of American National Standard for Information Sciences—Permanence of Paper for Printed Library Materials, ANSI/NISO Z39.48-1992.

FOR BILL

This, my premier book, is appropriately dedicated to my premier (and only) sweetheart. You've made my life sweet ever since I first knew you as that cute, quiet Billy in grade school. This book, along with so many wonderful blessings in my life, wouldn't have even been a thought in my head without you.

Contents

Foreword

Here in Virginia's Shenandoah Valley, we're not in a maple syrup region. Outside the Valley toward West Virginia, yes, but not here in the Valley. Yet when we arrived here in 1961, our yard had several sugar maples. Few trees exhibit such ornamental beauty during fall foliage brilliance.

Two were already more than twelve inches in diameter when we moved in and another two were saplings adjoining the garden plot. My older brother as a teenager decided to tap the two larger trees one year. I still remember being transfixed by the whole process. He made maple sugar rather than syrup that first year, and that quickly became my sweetener of choice. It still is today. He didn't continue the process every year because football, gymnastics, and regular school activities got in the way. We didn't tap those trees again for about twenty years.

By the time Teresa and I married and moved into the attic of the old farmhouse, the two bigger trees were magnificent eighteen-inch specimens and the two smaller ones along the garden had become healthy twelve-inchers. Our son, Daniel, became interested in sugaring as a pre-teen. After reading a book on the topic, he tapped all four trees and made a gallon and a half of syrup. We enjoyed it immensely. The next year he tapped our trees and a neighbor's trees. By the age of fourteen, he was tapping twenty or thirty in the community, and we had a metal fabricator put together a simple stainless steel evaporator pan for him.

Our family's devotion to entrepreneurism expressed itself in his liquid gold: Why not turn it into maple donuts and sell them at the local farmer's market? These donuts sensationalized the local market, garnering front page newspaper articles and all the exposure a fourteen-year-old could want. Enlisting the help of his younger sister in the kitchen, our two children cranked out dozens of maple donuts and padded their savings accounts substantially.

Today our apprentice manager Eric taps about a hundred trees within three miles of our farm and makes anywhere from twenty to thirty gallons of syrup a year, adding an entrepreneurial dimension to his farm leadership duties. What a delight, every spring, to see the entire community sprout with five-gallon buckets and taps along the roads, the lanes, and field edges. It's become one of our most enjoyable community-endearing

emotional equity bridges in the neighborhood: An area that is not on anyone's radar as a sugaring area.

Perhaps nothing is as viscerally seasonal as sap rising in trees. It's a rite of passage from winter to spring. However the act of sugarmaking can be enjoyed anywhere in the world, even in the tropics. Skeptics will find that and many more encouraging points in *Sweet Maple* by Michelle Visser. Too often we think sugaring is only a regional thing, limited to cold climates—but you can tap sycamore, birch, and even walnut trees. The boundless opportunity expressed in this handy do-it-yourself manual brings homestead sugaring into possibility for all of us. That is both empowering and liberating.

Unlike most homesteading and farming ventures, sugaring offers fast turnaround from work to reward, an ideal model for incentivizing children to join the enterprise. This book dares to question the refined white sugar industry. If thousands and thousands of people would tap their nearby trees, the collective sweetness would yield nutritional advantages as well as a fundamental shift in dependence on the sugar industry.

Speaking of nutrition, you'll find Michelle's research compelling. From quebecol, an anti-inflammatory and anti-carcinogen, to polyphenols that encourage brain health and deter diabetes, sweetness from tree sap is a completely different food critter than regular sugar and even honey. Tree sap is even indicated as an antidote to superbugs. While maple is and probably always will be the queen of the tree sap sweeteners, the same properties with taste permutations can be enjoyed by a host of different tree species.

Here at Polyface Farm Eric now collects more than a thousand gallons of sap a year and uses a genuine boiling pan with drain spigot and a nice sugar shack adjoining the garage. As Michelle eloquently notes, few things are as family-oriented as sugaring. From scouting for trees ("Look, Daddy, there's one!") to the magic of 219°F, few homestead enterprises yield such great memories. Certainly none yields such a great reward. Who doesn't love maple syrup? For a child, the whole process smacks of alchemy, of magic, of wonder and awe, and that's a good thing to add to any homestead family function.

If for no other reason than to root our youngsters in the mystery and practicality of participatory environmentalism, we should join the sugaring movement. We desperately need that in a day when our young people seldom have chores and stewardship responsibilities.

Sweet Maple is as much about how we can live as it is about converting sap into usable sweetener. Every member of Michelle's family is involved in these pages, making the book a compelling one for anyone's self-reliance book shelf. Tuning into the rhythms of our own nests is profoundly gratifying, and this book is a catalyst for enjoying the stewardship music.

—Joel Salatin, farmer and author
March 11, 2019

Acknowledgments

If you know anything about me, you probably know I'm a failure at many things. Indeed, I've failed very successfully at making backyard maple syrup as well as baking with maple syrup. It's the lessons I've learned in the midst of failing that make up the heart of these pages. Even so, this book would never have come to fruition had it not been for the help and encouragement of many others.

My daughters encouraged me to start writing about our homestead when they saw how content I was in our new home—a home which was actually "older than dirt," my momma would've said (yes, she did like her hyperboles).

So that first summer on our slowly forming, never-planned-for homestead, I started writing about my new life and joy, even in the midst of my ineptitude and continual learning curve. My daughters' encouragement birthed my blog SoulyRested.com.

Then winter arrived, with all 114 accumulated inches of beautiful snow and 2-foot-long glistening icicles. My husband Bill gave me a taste for maple when he tried tapping a few trees, including the stately sugar maple that was most likely planted 20 feet from our front door when George Washington or John Adams was president. Much more importantly, though, I need to acknowledge that Bill planted himself by my less-than-perfect side 25 years ago and has never considered uprooting, even though things weren't always "sweet."

The beautiful sugar maple in our front yard may have been planted when our house was built, around 1800.

In the end, all my acknowledgments come back to God who has given me even more than a supportive family, a rustic farmhouse on rolling acres, and a taste for an amazing all-natural sweetener that he directs to flow through my maple trees. He has given me a taste for simple joy. Nothing I do, from milking the cow, to gathering eggs, to writing this book, is worth doing without acknowledging him and tasting the simple joys he places in my days. In the end, our meager efforts to bottle homemade maple syrup are a testimony to the long hours of collection, late nights of boiling, and sweet depths of God's grace.

Introduction: Define the Simple Joys

Ever thought about trying to make your own maple syrup? Maybe you're just curious about the whole process. Maybe you know you're diving into it next winter, sink or swim, and you'd rather swim. Maybe you'd like a glimpse into our family's efforts to live life a little more simply by raising a few farm animals and making our own all-natural sugar. Or maybe you're longing to slow down just a bit and add a simple joy to your family's busy schedule. Something to help you stop whizzing through today, focused on the unimportant. In your hands you're holding a book about my family's failures (lots) and successes (a few) during our first few winters' attempts to turn tree sap into liquid-gold sweetness. I'm glad you're along for the ride.

Let's just get this out in the open. While I'm a colossal fan of maple—heck, if one can be a cheerleader for golden liquid sugar, then that's me—I'm not an expert sugarmaker. I sometimes burn my sap or lazily ignore the fact that I should calibrate my thermometer. I've even bottled at the wrong "Brix," which is a sugarmaker's measurement not to be ignored. The truth is, if I somehow make you think I'm an expert sugarmaker, you will quickly know I'm not. Heck, I mess up majorly at things I am kind of good at, so I have no room to project any expert image where I feel inadequate.

Take baseball, for example. I'm a huge fan, but I'm not an expert on the rules of the game. I could talk about the 2004 World Series with a deep, double-dimple smile, but I probably couldn't name more than half of this year's roster of my favorite team and I can't, for the life of me, understand the rules for an infield fly. I gave up trying. Still there aren't many things I'd rather do more than sit in the oldest seats in baseball with my daughters, hear the vendors calling out that dogs and cotton candy are near, and

The perfect place for four sisters to spend a sunny summer evening.

thrill at the deep crack that sends a ball soaring into an empty spot in the outfield—because I love the feel of baseball. The stories. The history. The sounds. I am an admirer and enthusiast of the game, but I'm not a baseball expert—not even by means of a far-reaching exaggeration.

In the same way I can enjoy America's favorite pastime without understanding the nuances of a drop third strike, I can certainly make some amazing maple syrup without being a professional sugarmaker. After all, when you boil it down to the basics (see what I did there?), maple syrup is a pretty simple idea and one we all learned in middle school. When you boil liquid—like tree sap—water evaporates and leaves behind a more concentrated liquid, like syrup.

As soon as you drill a little hole in a maple tree and wind up with a jar of liquid sugar, you'll realize there is so much more that you want to know. *Sweet Maple* is the result of what my family has learned so far about this glorious golden sweetener after a few New England winters spent tapping a few maple trees, boiling sap, and burning way too much to admit to. Even though my name is on the cover, our entire family is part of this sweet learning process. Even our daughter Logan, who was away studying mechanical engineering when my husband Bill tapped his first trees, got in on the action by completing a project about efficiency in the sugarbush. Kayla and Hayley, the two daughters currently living at home, have carried way more buckets of sap than I have, mainly because they are faster to get out in the cold than I am. I'll tell you about our other daughter Jordyn on page 39.

Carving out defining moments

While my goal in *Sweet Maple* is to help you find a tree to tap no matter where you live, show you how to turn sap into sugar, and convince you to give maple a starring role in your recipes, there's more in these pages for sure. In our "tips on tap," Bill and I answer the most common questions we get asked about sugaring and maple syrup. There are some nudges to get you to slow down and spend family time gathering sap and making syrup. I mean, sure, sugar making has provided delicious pancake breakfasts and helped our family consume less refined sugar, but if you asked me what it is about making maple syrup that has transformed my life? That's easy. Sugar making helps me define the important things.

You see, if I didn't have to venture out into our sugarbush on cold, gray days, I'd miss the joys that accompany an otherwise harsh winter. I'd miss the quiet stillness of snow-laden woods deep in restfulness, making me perfectly aware of every breath—in and out, in and out. I'd miss sightings of rabbits in their thick winter coats, scurrying under low branches of giant pines, and crimson flashes of a cardinal hopping among snow-heavy beech limbs. I know if I didn't have to leave the comforts of a cozy couch by a warm fire I wouldn't. Sugaring assures me that I'll not only catch glimpses of winter beauty and listen to my own thoughts, rising and lowering with my breath, but also enjoy the glory of the wood fire even more when I return to it.

The fact that I get to venture out into the sugarbush with my daughters and work with them to create something wonderful, well, that may be the sweetest reward. Maple scents the room; jars, lids, funnels, and filters are lined up; and amber bottles are filled in one fluid family effort. Come to think of it, maybe that's why my husband loves to give away our maple syrup to friends. He takes pride in the sweetness of not only the contents of the jar he's handing them, but also the moment he spent with his family to produce it on one cold, gray winter's night.

The kitchen is often a blur of activity and maple-scented steam when syrup reaches the perfect bottling temperature.

Hard work and simple joys

I've often wondered if we need the solitude and labor of an undertaking like sugaring now more than ever. Previous generations had so many things that required them to work hard—really hard—for simple joys. A brief look around my living room gives testament to this fact. My grandmother's wooden butter mold sits on my hearth. She would fill it with hand-churned butter for her children to spread on her homemade bread. Bill's grandmother's braided wool rug still cushions our feet more than eighty years after she cut each strip of wool by hand. I think about the quiet, reflective time all that churning and braiding required and realize I'm missing out.

Today our fast-paced society often denies us opportunities for solitude and sweat. Products and conveniences help us avoid both, but I think we miss out on so much by whizzing through each new day focused on the unimportant. For our family, backyard sugaring was part of a move away from suburbia to experience rural life. Sugaring offered us a delicious reason to slow down, be quiet together in the woods (or laugh together around the boiling sap), and work hard trudging through deep snow and carting buckets for the simple joy of it.

In addition to harvesting our own sugar from the woods, we grow as many of our own vegetables and fruit as possible, of which Kayla, my high school senior, is a master at preserving. I help, but she ultimately manages our canning afternoons. We raise a little of our own meat and eggs, with Hayley, my youngest (yet tallest) daughter, often organizing butchering days. We have lots of butter, yogurt, and ice cream when our cow Scout is in milk, although there never seems to be enough ice cream when Jordyn, my only one

After working together to carry full, heavy sap buckets uphill, friends enjoy time spent together around the dinner table even more.

in college this year, is home. Of course there isn't enough of anything, honestly, when college friends visit for the weekend.

All of these things ebb and flow on a homestead. I often think how odd it is that while real food is indeed seasonal, our society, for the sake of convenience, insists on having all flavors available at all times. We insist on excess, and no sweat. We insist on continual accessibility, and no inconvenience. We insist on ease and no hard work—but hard work makes a taste more desirable. It's the out-of-season time that makes ripe-off-the-vine taste more appealing. It's the eleven months of unavailability that makes just-picked food so delicious. It's the efforts—like those of my teens who are involved in preserving and processing our food—that make us appreciate our food and genuinely think about our choices. Sadly, we're out of sync with the seasonal nature of food, and we no longer even remember that effort should be required. The result? We've forgotten that food—real food—is wonderful.

As for maple? In my opinion, it's the best all-natural sweetener known to man. So I've included recipes oozing with naturally sweet deliciousness throughout this book. I hope you'll put them to work in your own kitchen.

As for homesteading? I've decided it's a rather personal thing, and we all define it a little differently. To me, homesteading is living a bit more simply, working a lot harder, and trying to do things just a little more like my parents did. Both my mom and dad were raised on rural farms in or near the West Virginia panhandle in the 1940s. Crazily enough, they were both one of 10 kids, and until I was in middle school I assumed everyone's parents were one of 10 farm kids.

I grew up hearing little stories about their simple lives that were huge, life-changing, and poignant for me. But their tales meant even more to me once I started living this homesteading life myself, just a few years ago. Through raising animals for meat, gathering daily eggs, and canning our harvest, I connected to Mom and Dad and my past in ways I never had before. I'm thankful I could enjoy that connection before they both passed away. It's a connection that I will cherish as the years widen.

I hope that as you read this book and learn about the fascinating intricacies of backyard maple syrup, you'll find a few of your own trees to tap or sweet maple-infused recipes to try. Life is too short not to notice some simple, defining moments every day, and some of them should be delicious. I've written *Sweet Maple* in hopes of bringing the joys of maple into homes across America, to assure people that it's okay that simple joys require hard work, and to bring the warm sweetness of an all-natural, super-food syrup into kitchens everywhere.

Poignant stories my parents told of their simple, agrarian childhoods meant even more to me once I started living this homesteading life myself.

Got Syrup?

BACKYARD SUGARING IS A LOGICAL FIRST STEP
TOWARD MORE SUSTAINABLE LIVING

While most folks can't own a family cow, almost everyone can tap a tree and have jars of their own amber syrup on their kitchen counter. The story of syrup starts in a tree during the warm months when we're busy sunbathing, eating fresh fruit, and vegetable gardening. In the summer trees are busy making natural sugar for themselves, thanks to that amazing process known as photosynthesis. When fall arrives, while we're preserving the harvest and stocking the barn with hay to feed the animals during the long winter months, a tree starts storing away sugar. All winter that wonderful sweetness is stored in the tree's inner bark as starch, just waiting until the tree is ready to work at new growth at the end of a long winter and needs some sugar again.

With the spring thaw, just as our hay reserves are depleted in the barn, wonderful enzymes in the tree do a magical thing by changing the starch back into sugar, which mixes with water that the tree has absorbed through its roots. The tree sends that wonderful sugar water up through its bark, and sugarmakers get busy. All a sugarmaker has to do is tap into some of that sap and boil it down to make syrup.

You might wonder how we did at our very first attempt at sugarmaking. We failed. We had awful sediment in the syrup. We boiled it too long. We boiled it too hot. We let it boil over. Again. And again. We didn't filter it. Then we filtered it, but incorrectly. Then we got the right kind of filter, but we didn't filter enough. Yes, we spent a lot of time and a fortune for eight dark, bitter, crystalized jars of syrup.

We bought books, scoured websites, watched videos, and tried and tried again. The next winter, we were armed with all we had learned by our own mistakes. We were

THOUGHTS OF COWS FROM CAMPUS

Logan, my oldest, was a mechanical engineering major at a rigorous college. Fortunately, she always had the simple joys of the farm to come home to.

Logan particularly adores farm babies, from bunnies to barn kitties to ducklings. She loved rehoming baby chicks one spring, from the incubator to under a broody hen, who became their momma. "But my biggest excitement was when I was the earliest riser and, checking on our pregnant Holstein, I discovered new-born Selah. I loved waking up the family with that news."

At first her friends thought it was odd that she'd ask about chickens or cows when she called home. But then they'd visit our homestead with her, and they'd start asking her about our chicken and cows when they saw her back on campus. The farm was a nice get-away for them.

Logan's favorite thing to do with maple?

"Honestly, my favorite thing to do with maple syrup is make it," she says. "I love going out in the woods and collecting sap and enjoy the satisfaction of lining up a dozen jars full of syrup."

much more successful, and the idea for this book took root. Now that we've reached the end of our third season of syrup making, and I've journaled, blogged, and written about the process, I know we still have more to learn. We have many ways we'd love to expand our own process, but for our little backyard production, we've reached the "we get it" stage. Well, at least until we burn another pan.

Is it worth all the hassle? We think so. Because in today's society, we've forgotten that real food is seasonal. Since food that's in season is always the best—for taste, texture, and nutritional value—we need to reconnect with this concept, and what sweeter way to do that than to tap a tree and boil some sugar?

It's not surprising that folks are longing to relearn the almost forgotten skills of older generations. Those talents, which now need instruction manuals, range from canning to beekeeping to—you guessed it—backyard sugarmaking. Many of my readers and blog followers from across the country all seem to agree that backyard sugaring is the logical next step in their family's quest for sustainable living, one rung on the ladder that's leading them to a simpler and healthier lifestyle. As Chrystal Smallwood, a reader in central Pennsylvania, explains of her newfound obsession with making maple syrup,

My favorite sugarmaker couldn't contain his sugar-making urges to just six short weeks out of the year, so we brought three bee hives onto the homestead too.

What parent wouldn't be enthusiastic to see teens interested in something sweet that harkens back to the days before social media and electronics?

"In my family's journey to live as sustainably as we can, it's incredibly satisfying to take this next step!"

As Christine Hutchinson, a reader from New York's Hudson Valley, points out, maple is a gentler alternative than honey. "I'm scared of bees! But I've been working to learn how to sustain myself for years. Sweeteners are one realm I have never tackled, but I'm eager to!" Here's a bonus for Christine and anyone who prefers maple over honey: Maple syrup offers fewer calories, 48 less, to be exact, in every ¼ cup.

For others, sugarmaking is the very first effort they have made toward anything resembling sustainability, but it seems like the perfect first step for them because, well, they have a tree and a bucket. Everyone to some degree longs for a more basic lifestyle, and parents are enthusiastic to see their children interested in anything that harkens back to the days before social media and electronics. Backyard sugarmaking is "a great activity to do as a family," Caylin Muehlberg in Minnesota points out, because "it teaches dedication to hard work and the literal 'sweet' rewards that can result."

From young children to senior citizens, the fascination with all-natural sugar—from tap to table—is widespread. Virginia Laycock, in west central Indiana, didn't tap her first tree until she was sixty-five. In fact, she doesn't even tap her own trees. She explains, "I got two turkey

To some degree, everyone longs for a more basic lifestyle.

fryers and asked my neighbors up and down the road if I could tap their trees. No one has ever told me 'no.' I share the syrup with those who share their tree with me. Making my own syrup is one of the most enjoyable things I have ever done."

A new generation of sugarmakers is emerging, and it's a logical response, as everyone is realizing the harsh impact that a fast-paced life, and poor food choices, has made on our society.

How we got started

When fall rested her full weight on the New Hampshire Lakes Region a few Octobers ago, we walked our woods and marked our sugar maples that were crowned in vibrant golden leaves. This was years ago, before "maple" was trending. As I watch maple replace pumpkin as the popular flavor of fall in nearby coffee shops, I realize we were trendy before the nation jumped on the maple bandwagon. Yep, our maple syrup operations manager—aka Bill—was ahead of the curve. He was hooked after making his first jar of syrup, even though it was dark and crystalized.

During the first year of our syrup escapades, we tapped only a handful of maple trees, with short tubing running from the trees directly into buckets at their base. By the second year, our maple syrup operations manager had bigger plans. The fact that we own fourteen wooded acres on a rocky New England hillside, that a nice portion of those trees are sugar maples, and that hillsides slope downward, gave Bill the urge to get a little more professional with our tapping in our second year of sugarmaking.

Walking the property

While we didn't know yet if we truly would run syrup tubing from tree to tree down the hillside, we had big dreams. So we walked the woods and marked what looked to us like the most promising trees while they still held their leaves, so it would be easy to identify the sugar maples.

We traversed our woods that evening: my high school sweetheart with a can of fluorescent spray paint, me with my camera, and Bixby (our labradoodle) with unbridled excitement. Our orange "x"s were marks of the potential sweet syrup we hoped to slather on French toast, use in baking, and add to our tea and hot chocolate the whole next year.

If you want to sell organic syrup, opt out of using spray paint on your trees. Try bright surveyors tape instead.

After we finished marking the maples, we moved on to all the exciting efforts that autumn ushers in on a farm. We canned tomatoes, salsa, and beans; pureed and froze pumpkin; and harvested our apples for pies and cider.

We are blessed to live in a colonial Cape Cod farmhouse that was built around 1800, complete with an old Rumford cooking fireplace with a brick oven on the side, which bakes breads and pizzas that make my heart sing (see the recipe for our favorite bread on page 28).

As winter settled in, the firewood was stacked high and we were enveloped in the white serenity that always accompanies a New England winter. My favorite part of that winter? The sight of our orange "x"s in the woods and thoughts of sugary sweetness to come.

Deciding if your area is good for tapping

Do you live in an area where late winter temperatures stay below freezing all night, many nights in a row, and then rise to the forties during the day? Then you're in prime maple syrup country. Here's the shocker: This isn't an iron-clad requirement for backyard sugarmaking. I grew up in the mid-Atlantic area and I could have definitely tapped some trees, even though I always thought it was something that could only be done in the far north. Truth be told, unusual weather fronts can produce wonderful sap runs, even in areas that are not typically cold enough for sugarmaking.

If you think you might like to try your hand at the whole sweet process and make your own maple syrup, you need to start by learning what trees are tappable, identifying and marking your trees, and then gathering the supplies you'll need. Read on for more information.

Identifying maple trees

The best trees for making syrup are sugar, black, red, and silver maples. Once you've studied the bark patterns of those maples, as well as their leaf shape and type of samaras (or the "whirly-birds," as my girls called them when they were little), you're ready to walk your property and find your maple trees. These illustrations will get you started, and you can take along one of a few helpful apps on your phone like PlantSnap or PictureThis.

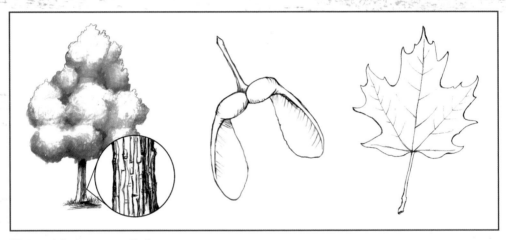

Sugar maple bark, samara, and leaf

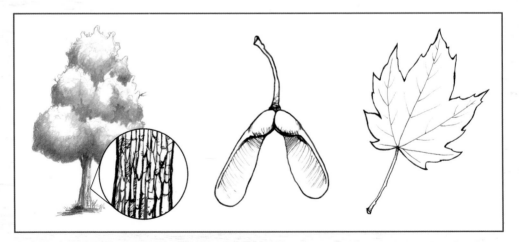

Red maple bark, samara, and leaf

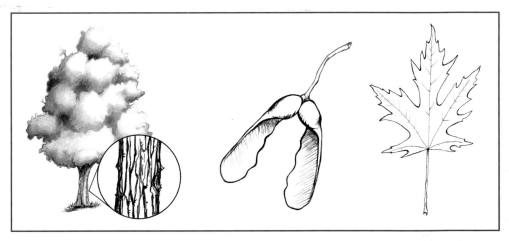

Silver maple bark, samara, and leaf

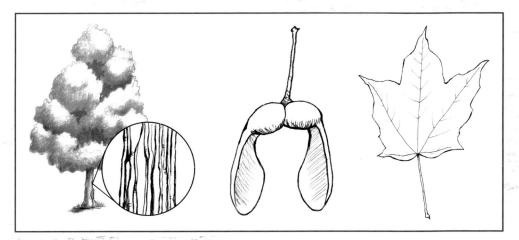

Black maple bark, samara, and leaf

Sugar maples are the holy grail of sap collection. They produce the largest quantity and sweetest quality of sap of any tree. Even so, if you don't have a productive maple to tap, there are twenty-nine sources of amazing all-natural syrup described in chapter 5. You might even have access to sweet syrup right now and not know it!

Knowing which maples to mark

You want the tree to be at least 10 inches in diameter. You also want to consider where the tree is on your property, how hard it is to access, and how much sun exposure it has. If it's in the heart of a wooded area, as so many of our maples are, it will not always provide sap on the same days as other maples that are more exposed to the warmth of the afternoon sun. The trees in the woods tend to produce later in the season than trees in open, sunny areas, so you may want to intentionally tap trees with varying sun exposure if you'd like to stagger your daily allotment of sap. You could also intentionally place your taps on different sides of the trees, with some facing morning sun and others, evening sun.

During our first year of tapping, we naively thought all maple trees would make great amounts of syrup. Boy, were we wrong. For reasons often unknown, some trees are workhorses. Sometimes the unassuming, barely 10-inch-diameter trees produce the most sap, while others (even the stately looking ones) turn out to be "duds" as Hayley calls them. At the end of sugaring season, mark your trees so you remember which ones you want to tap again and which ones might not be worth your time. Of course, you may want to give a "dud" another chance, because this year's dud could be next year's treasure tree. Bill and I do a lot of our sugaring together, but we also have our own areas of expertise. Me? I'm a maple addict. I love the byproducts of sugar-making, and I love baking with maple. So I let Bill take on the title of "primary sugarmaker" on our homestead. He deserves any title he wants for putting up with my shenanigans for 25 years. In exchange, Bill carries more buckets and spends more time at the evaporator than I do. I, on the other hand, eat

> **BILL'S TIP ON TAP**
> **Do I really need to follow certain tapping standards?**
>
> *Well, if I hope to tap a forest for a few decades, I have to be wise. If I tap trees that are too small, or overtap bigger trees, I may hurt my future productivity. If I think a tree looks at least 10 inches in diameter and it's healthy, I'll tap it. While the Maple Research Center in Vermont quotes 12 inches as the minimum, many other reliable studies have shown that 10 inches is reasonable. However if you tap small trees, you're removing a higher proportion of the carbohydrates they need. Give smaller trees a few more years to grow.*

more maple cream and maple sugar than he does. So, yeah, it's a pretty sweet arrangement.

Throughout the book, Bill puts on his "sugarmaker" hat to answer the more technical questions about tapping. I, on the other hand, don't wear hats often (unless it's my favorite base-ball team's hat). I'll answer the other questions.

Marking your trees

If you have a somewhat large area of trees you're marking, it helps to make a simple map of the trees' locations. We then spray paint a fluorescent orange "x" on the bark of each worthy tree (don't worry, it fades by springtime). You could also twist a bright-colored plastic, fabric, or string tie around the trunks or on large, low branches. Bright surveyors tape is ideal. I wouldn't recommend thin ties or yarn. Been there, done that. We marked dozens of sugar maples with bright yellow yarn one fall and realized by December most of the yarn had faded and broken off. The trees were impossible to find.

Of course if you have only one or two tappable trees, you won't need to mark them at all.

Gathering your sap collecting supplies

Once you've identified and marked your trees, you'll want to start gathering your supplies, so you're ready to tap the trees when the time is right. (For us, in New England, that varies each year, but often we find the best time to tap is a six-week window from late February through mid-April.) These are the supplies you'll need on hand as soon as the sap starts flowing:

Cordless drill. Okay, a cordless drill is not totally necessary if you want to do things the old-fashioned way with a hand drill, but it sure makes the job go faster.

Drill bits. Depending on the type of tap you're using, you'll want either a $5/16$ or $7/16$ drill bit to make the hole in your tree.

The maple branch on the right has opposite branches. The beech branch on the left has alternate branches.

Taps (or "spiles"). For taps, you have many options, and folks seem to prefer slightly different sizes. You can choose between ³⁄₁₆-, ¼-, and ⁵⁄₁₆-sized taps.

Hooks or plastic tubing. Hooks are attached to the spiles (some taps have a built-in hook), for hanging the bucket. We choose to sit our buckets on the ground and feed ⁵⁄₁₆ inch tubing from the tap into the buckets.

Bags. Some folks prefer plastic collection bags over buckets. Gerald Peterson is a self-proclaimed "small-scale suburban mapler" in Cedar Falls, Iowa, who likes using bags. "They're surprisingly strong, and I like that we can tell how full they are at a glance. Plus, there's nothing to clean up or store off-season."

Buckets. We like using food-grade 5-gallon buckets with lids. We found ours (often even with predrilled holes in the lids for the tubing) at a local grain and food store. Of course, when you live in the country, nothing is actually close by, so we've ordered them online at great prices as well. Deli or donut shops may be willing to give you food-grade buckets for free if they often have their ingredients delivered in them. It's worth asking. After talking to Pete Roth, a maple syrup pro in

Pete Roth grew up in a sugarhouse and still today there's no place he'd rather be.

SWEET SUGGESTIONS FROM A SUGARMAKER

Pete Roth doesn't remember a day not spent near a sugarbush. In fact, the first time I talked to Pete, he told me, "I grew up in a box in a corner of the sugarhouse." The way he delivered the line made me immediately confident that it's his own personal tagline in life. After his dad, John Roth, tapped his first tree in 1956, the whole family was hooked, even the unborn members, including Pete.

Pete's advice?
Don't cut corners on the important stuff. "You're making a food item here, so please respect that."

Pete's equipment recommendation?
"You can buy food-grade buckets online for a steal, and you need to be boiling in a nice stainless steel pan, with no soldering or welding."

Pete's favorite recipe?

Sweet Maple Salami
1. Slice 16 ounces of smoked salami into bite-sized pieces.
2. Cook them in a large skillet, over medium heat.
3. Add 1½ cups of maple syrup and bring to a slow, rolling boil. Reduce heat to low and simmer for about 20 minutes. You'll see the salami caramelize in the skillet. (In a slow cooker, cook the meat and syrup on low for 2 hours.)

BILL'S TIP ON TAP
Should I collect sap in bags or buckets?

We prefer buckets. Bags tend to attract bothersome squirrels who want a taste. Buckets hold more, have lids that effectively keep the critters out, and are great for storing sap. We move full buckets to a snow bank and/or a well shaded area to keep sap cold until we're ready to boil. We prefer white buckets over darker colored ones because they keep the sap cooler on a sunny day and are almost translucent, so we can tell how much sap is inside.

MICHELLE'S TIP ON TAP
What if I don't collect enough sap to make syrup?

Sap is a refreshing, antioxidant-filled drink. You can also use maple sap to make coffee and tea, and even brew beer with it I'm told. In fact, you can use maple sap in any recipe that calls for water.

Wisconsin, I realized reusing buckets isn't always the best bet. You see, Pete stopped purchasing sap from backyard sugarmakers because so many were bringing him sap in used containers that had previously housed pickles or jalapeño peppers. No matter how well you scrub a bucket, one that once held dill pickles will never be suited for maple sap—unless you happen to prefer dill-flavored maple over regular-old delicious.

Holding tanks. If you'll be collecting many gallons of sap every day, you may want to look into food-grade holding tanks as well. When our number of taps exceeded a few dozen, we started collecting some in tanks, with tubing connecting the trees to our tank.

I had originally thought we could save money on buckets all together by using modified milk jugs, but I can honestly say my husband was right about the craziness of that idea. From our most productive trees, we can gather 5 gallons of sap in only half a day. A milk jug would have never been big enough. All that sap would have been wasted, spilling onto the ground before I got around to collecting it. Of course, if you want to do more than just collect maple sap, you'll also need sap processing equipment. (More on that in the following chapters.)

MAPLE SANDWICH BREAD

This bread has a surprisingly warm, sweet maple taste that no one in my house can resist. It's delicious toasted and paired with maple-infused butter (see recipe on page 35). It also makes crazy yummy ham sandwiches. It will keep well for three to five days on the counter in an air-tight container. You could also freeze it for longer storage, but honestly, in our house it's always devoured quickly.

2 cups boiling water

1 cup rolled oats (we use traditional, but I'm told quick oats are fine)

½ cup maple syrup

1 tablespoon honey

¼ cup butter

2½ teaspoon salt

1 teaspoon cinnamon

1 tablespoon instant yeast

5½ cups flour

1. Combine the water, oats, syrup, honey, butter, salt, and cinnamon in a large bowl.

2. Let cool about 15 minutes then add the yeast and flour, stirring to form dough.

3. Knead by hand for about 10 minutes until the dough is satiny. Place your dough in a lightly greased bowl and cover it with a thin towel. Let it rise for an hour in a warm area that is free of drafts.

4. Divide the risen dough in half, shape it into two loaves, and place them in greased bread pans. Cover pans with lightly greased plastic wrap and allow the loaves to rise until they've crowned about 1 inch over the rims of the pans, which typically takes another 60–90 minutes.

5. Preheat oven to 350°F. Bake the loaves for 35–40 minutes, covering them lightly with aluminum foil the last 10–15 minutes to prevent over-browning.

YIELDS TWO 9X5-INCH LOAVES

MAPLE BISCUITS

We have a binder in our kitchen filled with recipes that Kayla assembled half a decade ago. This is one of them. Yes, Kayla was always a little obsessive, even as a child. Of course, there's an added bonus if the recipe uses something we're drowning in on any given season on the farm such as foamy cream. If you don't have fresh cream, or any heavy cream at all, substitute ¾ cup whole milk and ¼ cup melted butter for every 1 cup of cream. These biscuits are also yummy with 2 tablespoons of maple sugar in place of the maple syrup, or even whole cane sugar or refined sugar if you don't have maple on hand. Just up your amount of cream a little until your consistency is right.

6 cups flour
2 tablespoons maple syrup
2 tablespoons baking powder
1½ teaspoons salt
2 cups cream, or more as needed
Additional maple syrup for basting

1. Pre-heat oven to 425°F.

2. In a large bowl, whisk together flour, syrup, baking powder, and salt.

3. Add 2 cups of cream (or ½ cup melted butter and 1½ cups whole milk) to the flour mixture, mixing with a wooden spoon or your hands, until a soft, wet dough forms. Add up to 1 additional cup of cream, gradually, if needed.

4. Push the dough out with your hands on a floured surface until about 1¼ inch thick. Cut out as many biscuits as you can, then gather the scraps, knead them together, and re-push out and re-cut. You can do this as many times as you need to. At this point, if you'd rather freeze the biscuits for later, see details on the next page.

5. Reduce temperature to 400°F when you put the biscuits in the oven. Bake for 15–20 minutes, basting them with a second delicious coating of maple syrup a minute or two before removing them from the oven.

YIELDS 20–24 BISCUITS

MAPLE FREEZER BISCUITS

While we love fresh biscuits with a good meat-and-potatoes meal, we're not always too crazy about the added effort of making biscuits. So when we have the extra time, Kayla and I will mix up a double batch of Maple Biscuits and freeze them. I can't tell you how many times I've been twenty minutes away from serving a large, delicious meal, only to realize I totally forgot bread or rolls, and I've been so thankful I could add homemade biscuits to the menu with no preparation.

12 cups flour
4 tablespoons maple syrup
4 tablespoons baking powder
3 teaspoons salt
4 cups cream

1. In a large bowl, whisk together flour, syrup, baking powder, and salt.

2. Add 4 cups of cream (or 1 cup melted butter and 3 cups whole milk) to the dry ingredients, mixing with a wooden spoon or your hands, until a soft, wet dough forms. Add another cup or two of cream, gradually, if needed.

3. Push the dough out with your hands on a floured surface until about 1¼ inch thick. Cut out as many biscuits as you can, using a square or round cookie cutter. For that matter, you can use any shape cookie cutter you like. I avoid using a glass because the dull edges of the rim leads to biscuits that don't rise as well.

4. Gather the scraps, knead them together, and re-push out and re-cut. You can do this as many times as you need.

5. Place the biscuits on a greased cookie sheet, cover them with a thin towel, and put them in the freezer for a few hours until they're frozen. Then move them to a large resealable, freezer-safe bag, or an air-tight container, and put them back in the freezer until you're ready to bake them.

YIELDS 3–4 DOZEN BISCUITS

Sweeten up any biscuit with some maple.

Don't hesitate to brush on some maple to any bread or biscuit recipe you make. Feel free to lightly baste before baking and again a few minutes before they're ready to come out of the oven. It's a super easy way to upgrade any bread to sweet and delicious.

MAPLE-INFUSED BUTTER

While you certainly could simply butter your bread and then drizzle some maple syrup right on top for an extra special treat at any meal, I prefer this maple-infused option. When I take the time to grind my own flour and make homemade bread, I am always eager to top it with this butter. Grinding your own flour is a piece of cake . . . or it makes a piece of cake . . . or maybe I just have cake on the brain. The resulting bread, slathered in some maple-infused butter? Well, that's infused with mmm.

½ **cup unsalted butter**

2 **tablespoons brown sugar**

2 **tablespoons maple syrup**

½ **teaspoon cinnamon**

1. Place the butter in your mixer, fresh out of the fridge if you don't mind lumpy butter. If you'd like extra smooth butter, use the butter at room temperature. Add other ingredients, mix, and serve.

2. If you have 30 minutes to spare and want to refrigerate the butter, you can form it into a nice stick or ball shape as well.

YIELDS ½ CUP OF BUTTER

Tap Well

GO AHEAD . . . TAP A TREE
AND SEE WHAT IT GETS YOU

Throughout February, fresh snow graces the ground most days on our New England homestead. If we're abundantly "blessed" with the white stuff, we get plenty of exercise shoveling the drive and raking the roof. Yes, we literally rake our roof when the snow piles up too deep, otherwise the weight would cave a roof. Some days I even trudge out through to the finch house to rake the bird's roof too, to keep it nice until they're ready to move back up north in the spring.

Once I'm bundled up and outside I'm usually grateful for the excuse to be out. Plus I know I'll appreciate the warmth even more when I return to it. In fact, most days I'm thankful that the continual snowfall offers a new white cloak to our tired, old, red cape that has nestled in this diminutive neck of the woods for centuries.

Yes, our family is tucked away by the fire as much as possible on chilly February days. When the temperature starts to climb, the sun does linger a little longer on the days she chooses to show herself in the blue-gray sky, and the sap in all our maples starts a celebratory spring-is-on-her-way promenade. The previous fall, every tree wisely started to conserve. Knowing the cold, long, dark nights of December and January were coming, trees held back their sugar in October. Instead of sending the food to their branches and leaves, deciduous roots everywhere started to tuck away their food supply for when the tree would need it the most. Just as Kayla and I were canning our garden vegetables and stocking our pantry shelves, maples, beech, walnuts, and sycamores everywhere were also harvesting and prepping for winter. They were turning their sugar into starch to store in their roots for promising daytime temperatures that signal it's time to start

nourishing the branches, turning the stored starch into sugar and sending it up the tree so the buds can grow, so the summer leaves can grow, so the sun's heat can warm the leaves and make more sugar.

This time of year without fail, while we're tucked away from February winds, our family starts dreaming of homemade maple syrup. So, like it or not, we venture out into the cold evenings. We start the process of running a new stretch of alluring sky-blue colored sap lines for when the sap starts to wake up each day.

Surely one of these years we will be content with the number of maples we have run lines to. Surely one of these years we will say, "Yep, last year's amount of syrup was perfect," and we'll be content. I don't know when that year will arrive, and until it does, there are always more trees to tap.

THE HERO ON OUR HOMESTEAD

Jordyn is our second daughter, but really she's my hero. Diagnosed with an unusual neurological condition called Complex Regional Pain Syndrome (CRPS), she spent her twentieth birthday, and many more weeks, in the ICU and a clinical trial.

Yet years of excruciating pain, surgery, and an artificial plastic disc made her an expert on difficulty at an age when most girls are worrying about picking a prom dress. CRPS may have left Jordyn with life-long burning sensations in her left foot, but alongside the pain, she developed an attitude toward appreciating daily joys in ways I have yet to master.

How has the homesteading life helped her? Jordyn says, "The animals were therapeutic for me during some really bad years. I fall in love with at least one particular baby chick every spring. When there are baby rabbits, well, they get pretty comfy in my room whenever I can sneak one or two by Mom. If only I could sneak Selah, our baby cow, upstairs."

Jordyn's favorite thing to do with maple?

Jordyn loves maple the best when it's infused in a tall cone of maple cotton candy. She explains, "All good New England fairs have it. I'm still trying to convince Mom and Dad they need their own cotton candy machine."

Some first-year mistakes

That first maple-syrup February, we tapped about a dozen trees. I had envisioned quaint tin buckets hanging from silver spouts here and there throughout our woods. That was my first mistake. Turns out those quaint options are much more expensive and not nearly as practical as good-old food-grade plastic buckets. Good thing my pragmatic husband took on the job of picking up our supplies.

Then I thought if we were just going to use "ugly" buckets, why not clean out milk jugs to use for free collection containers? That was my second mistake. Tiny jugs would have wound up wasting gallons of precious sap a day on the good days.

We simply drilled a hole, attached tubing to the taps, and ran the tubing into lidded buckets at the base of the trees. Then we had to empty the buckets when they were full, store the sap somewhere cool until we were ready to boil it (we used extra buckets and a giant cooler for storage), and then cart the syrup to our propane-fired cooking pot when we were ready to boil some down.

It pretty much took us all day to boil it down. If we overfilled the pot or left it unattended for too long, it would foam up and over the pot. (Later, I'll explain what we learned during our second year of production that enabled us to cut the time and money required to boil down the sap in half.)

MICHELLE'S TIP ON TAP

How do you keep sap from boiling over?

If you toss in a tablespoon of butter or rub it around the pot's rim, the crazy bubbles and foam magically dissipate.

tip

We learned that bucket transportation can get a little cumbersome when more than a dozen buckets have to be carted around at one time. Because we didn't feel like doing all that cumbersome lugging, we didn't always check the buckets daily, which led to the occasional waste of precious sap when it overflowed. That was a huge mistake.

Even worse, we didn't realize how detrimental a slightly warm, sunny day could be for sap sitting in a bucket. Mind you, I use the term "warm" rather loosely. I am talking "warm" in terms of a New England day in March. But even on a 40- to 45-degree day,

Bacteria love sugar. The jar on the right is fresh from the tree. The jar on the left has set too long at room temperature and needs to be thrown away.

sap can get too warm. We mistakenly let it sit for a few sunny days in a row and had to throw away buckets full of precious sap. That was one of the biggest mistakes of all.

If the sap gets warm while you're storing it, it will turn cloudy. Because sap is basically sugar water, it is a perfect home for bacterial growth. So even slightly cloudy sap needs to be disposed of.

More teachable moments

Fast forward to the following winter. In early February, we knew that soon the days would warm up just enough for the sap to embark on a slow dance down the tree tubing that's hidden away under the bark. We also knew that if we were smart enough to tap into the right trees, at the right place, in the right way, we could become part of the beautifully tasty dance.

We were extra excited because our backyard production was going a bit "uptown." We "inherited" large collection tanks from a greenhouse that was upgrading theirs. The only downside? The two 80-gallon tanks were 400 miles south of our homestead. Until we could make the trek to pick them up, many weeks later, we worked on installing as much tubing as possible in early February. (I should insert a word of warning here: I'd never consider reusing a storage container for sap unless I know its full history. In this case, only water had been stored in these tanks.)

Thanks to our new holding tanks, we thought we would be able to forgo the daily round up and carting of heavy buckets in exchange for tubing that, once installed, would let us gather much more sap with much less effort.

Knowing the sap would surprise us and start flowing suddenly, almost unexpectedly, we started running our collection tubing the first Saturday morning in February, with more than 12 inches of snow on the ground. Another big snow storm was headed our way, so we tried to install as much tubing as we could. Bill, Kayla, Bixby, and I were all excited to run our first sap lines. Bill was excited to try out the ingenious-looking gripper that he intended to use at the beginning of our main line of tubing. The piece looked so nifty. (I mean who wouldn't like a giant Chinese finger trap holding his tap lines?) But he couldn't get it to work well and reverted to old-fashioned cutting and wrapping of wire.

Some appealing gadgets, like this tension grip, wind up in the trash. It's always wise to ask seasoned sugarmakers before investing in a gizmo you may not need.

Often ingenuity serves a sugarmaker best. More often than not, most backyard sugarmakers can make many DIY alternatives, like simple wrapped wire and eyelets, to suit their needs.

Bill's creation is an ingenious help with the tubing.

We installed a ¾-inch main line down the wide path that runs up the back of our property. It works out nicely that our property stretches uphill through the woods, so gravity is our friend in our sugar making efforts. It also came in handy that Bill built a tubing reel from scraps he pulled together and a little ingenuity. The tubing is cumbersome and awkward if you're trying to carry, wrap, and unwrap it in the woods. You can purchase some neat contraptions for this purpose, but Bill's always been one to enjoy an engineering challenge. We're a nice team, he and I. While I build thoughts with written words, he builds gadgets with scraps.

If you don't have maples in rows on a sloped area, you can use short pieces of tubing to connect each tap to a large, lidded bucket on the ground. If you have a handful of maples that aren't on a sloped area but are growing in somewhat of a line, you could gradually lower your tap placement from one tree to the next, to allow gravity to still feed the sap through the tube.

> **BILL'S TIP ON TAP**
>
> **I struggle with carrying and unwinding tubing in the woods when I'm running new lines. Any tips?**
>
> *I hate dealing with tubing! I found a gizmo that would help, but man, it was expensive. So I designed and built my own homemade tubing reel, and life is a lot easier now.*

BILL'S TIP ON TAP

I have the worst time connecting my tubing. Any suggestions?

We struggled with this problem for years until I figured out that hot water causes the tubing to expand, allowing the connectors to smoothly fit right in. I carry a thermos of hot water with me in the woods when I'm running my tubing. An even easier option, if you want to spend a little more money on your hobby, is to purchase a tool just for this purpose.

We planned to end the tubing in our large inherited water collection tanks not too far from our barn. If I'm honest, I didn't really think it through. I thought I'd be carting fewer buckets of sap that winter. In reality, because we didn't have a tractor that could hold the buckets, I was carrying more buckets than the year before. Even though the tubing was bringing all the sap to one central location, that location was still many hundred feet from our boiling location. So the work actually increased that year, because we needed to siphon

You'll want a nice, steady drop in your lines to encourage a natural vacuum.

out the sap into buckets. Then we were still carrying the buckets of sap to the boiling area. Someday, once we have a tractor or 4-wheeler to help with the work, we'll simply pump the sap in the tanks on the ground into tanks on our tractor, which we can drive right up to our processing area.

Meanwhile, another 15 inches of snow had dropped since we started installing our lines. More than two feet of snow has a way of hampering progress. But we were able, little by little, to install one small section of tubing at a time. We connected maples in perpendicular lines, with 5/16-inch tubing, to our original, 3/4-inch main tube. Thankfully the weather stayed cold and our makeshift bucket system never overflowed. We didn't have to learn any hard lessons this time, but we could have easily had a wasteful problem on our hands, because we had numerous trees tapped but nothing to collect their sap in for many long February weeks.

Our thoughts on smaller tubing

The lesson we have learned after the fact (it figures, right?) is that a smaller diameter tubing will be much more efficient at creating a natural vacuum in the line. So next year we plan on using 3/16-inch tubing in new areas that we tap. Our hope is that our 3/16-inch lines will always be full, and full lines create a natural suction, so even more sap will be pulled from each tree. (Bonus is that the 3/16-inch tubing warms up faster

and is slower to freeze.) Fancy operations have vacuum pumps set up that allow the sugarmakers to see 29in of vacuum. With an efficient 3⁄16-inch tubing set up, backyard sugarmakers like us are reporting as high as 23in of vacuum. Not bad considering that 3⁄16-inch tubing is cheaper than the larger stuff and there's no need to purchase a vacuum pump to get the 23in of vacuum.

Of course, if you're considering installing lines, no matter what size you use or how you install them, keep in mind that you will need to make a habit of walking the lines often and checking for damage caused by squirrels, woodpeckers, falling branches, and other potential problems.

So you want to run some lines?

If you're going to make the effort, you might as well make sure you're creating a natural vacuum in your lines. Here are some tips to keep in mind:

- Use the smallest diameter tubing you can. The larger diameter line you use, the more taps are needed to achieve a vacuum.

- Count your taps. If you use 3⁄16-inch tubing, you'll want 20–25 taps on each section of line. You'll want a minimum of a 20-foot drop from the top tap to the bottom one, where your 3⁄16-inch meets up with your mainline.

- Keep it short and sweet when you can. The longer your span of tubing in any section, the lower vacuum you'll have.

- Go deep when you can. The steeper drop you have, the more vacuum you'll have.

- Be consistent. Your vacuum will be most effective with a continual slope of at least 15 percent.

- Make it tight. You'll need to walk your lines often, looking (and listening) for leaks.

- Avoid any sags or sharp zig zagging in your line, especially in shallow-sloped areas if you want optimal performance.

- Take your time. Plan out your lines before you even start, or you may wind up with a mess.

- Support your main line. Run a cable that you can use to connect your main line to, so it's well supported if you get wet, heavy snowfall.

If you're considering purchasing a pump, the coop extension at the University of New Hampshire offers these guidelines: "A vacuum pump's capacity is measured by how much air it can move in a certain amount of time—cubic feet per minute (CFM). For every 100 taps in tubing system, a pump with 1 to 1½ CFM is needed. If 500 taps are on vacuum, a pump with a capacity of 5 to 7.5 CFM is needed."

Sugarmaker Ryan Browne, of Rising Sun Farm, recommends that you don't write off a used option. "You can sometimes find a great used pump for a great price." (Meet Ryan on page 117.)

What really happens when we tap a tree?

Wood is made up of a lot of fibers, which are actually dead cells with extra-thick walls that have a very important purpose, even though they are no longer living. These fibers make the wood strong. The "plumbing system" of the tree weaves around and in between those fiber cells. It's not a system of long "pipes" that extend directly from the roots to the leaves. Instead, the "plumbing" vessels are each about an inch long and very narrow. Millions of them connect one to another all along the height of a tree and allow sap to flow throughout—up and down as well as side-to-side. Also tucked among the thick-walled fiber cells and the mini tubes are living cells. These living cells store starch. The leaves make this starch via photosynthesis in the spring and summer, and the tree uses the starch for energy to grow. At certain temperatures, the starch converts to sucrose (thank goodness for maple syrup lovers) and some flows into the sap in the mini tubes.

So what happens when we tap into a tree? We're punching a small, permanent hole that is impossible to see on the outside within just a few years, because new growth begins to cover the hole with repair tissue before sugaring season ends. Inside the tree, on the other hand, there is always evidence that we've drilled the hole. A permanent stain forms around the tap hole that signifies the "plumbing" vessels that existed around that tap are now permanently plugged and those living cells are now dead cells. The wood itself is not decayed, simply stained, and no damage occurs anywhere in the tree beyond that small, stained area. The tree compartmentalizes the damage. As long as sugarmakers practice wise tapping procedures, a maple tree will heal itself and continue producing wonderful sap to turn into syrup for centuries.

Questions to ask yourself before tapping your trees

In general, maple producers follow tapping guidelines—unofficial practices that make sure the delicious art of sugarmaking remains sustainable. As I researched all we needed to know before tapping our trees, I decided these 10 questions are the important ones to ask yourself.

1. Do I live in syrup country?

Getting productive amounts of sap from trees is not really based on your latitude or longitude as much as on your seasonal weather. If you live where there is a seasonal freeze and thaw cycle, you can be a sugarmaker (even if you don't have maples! See chapter 5).

Even so, the more I researched, the more intrigued I was to meet plenty of folks who tap in very nontraditional places. For example, despite common theories about the need for freezing temperatures, some sugarmakers on Vancouver Island have been tapping big-leaf maples for over a decade and learning that trees are not always predictable based on the thermometer alone. Members of the Vancouver Island Sapsuckers syrup-making group explain that in the Pacific Northwest, winter storms coming in off the ocean cause such a change in high and low fronts that trees may gush sap after a snowstorm, even though temperatures may never dip below freezing.

So, no, you don't need freezing temperatures or sugar maples to try your hand at making some syrup. If anyone asks me if it's worth a try, I never hesitate to encourage them to tap a tree and see what it gets them.

2. When should I tap?

Alternating freezing and thawing temperatures are usually necessary to create pressure in the tree, which causes the sap to flow when you tap into it. Sap runs best when temperatures drop below freezing at night and rise into the 40s during the day. For optimal tree health, it's best to wait patiently until temperatures are at least slightly above freezing on the day you do your tapping. In cold regions it's seldom time to tap before late February. It takes an extended period of warmer temperatures for the sap to thaw.

If there's a lot of snow shoveling in your forecast, you're most likely better off waiting to tap your trees.

One year we just couldn't wait. My favorite sugarmaker tapped a handful of trees in mid-January because it turned unusually warm for a few days, and he was itching to get started making syrup. We made one quart of syrup. One. Then we had two more big snow storms before mid-February, and there we were with our single, small jar of syrup and not one more drop of sap. At that point, we put in lots more taps and thought spring was arriving early. Then we had two more snow storms. We did a lot more shoveling. We soon realized that those January taps weren't a good idea because by mid-March when sugaring was at its peak here in New England, those early taps were scarred over and not giving us any sap. Yes, we could have drilled new holes on those trees Bill tapped too early, but we'd be putting a lot of wear and tear on our sugarbush if we did such non-sense to all the trees every year. In the end, we probably missed out on gallons' worth of syrup that those trees would have produced if we had just waited patiently another month or so to tap.

I should say, though, in warmer areas, weather fluctuations may happen throughout the winter, and optimal sap flow may be in January, so no matter where you live it's not a bad idea to be ready in January and watch the extended forecast. If you have a lot of trees, you could even tap a test tree, to see exactly what the sap flow is like every day.

I'll fess up here—this topic had me baffled and I wondered why it mattered. I mean, why not drill a hole in January and just watch occasionally for sap in your bucket? Then if sap didn't flow until March, no biggie, right? That way at least we wouldn't miss any opportunity for sap if we did have a few perfect days early on. What I didn't understand was how efficiently a tree heals itself. As soon as you tap your first hole, the tree starts repairing the damage. Once you drill your hole, you have a limited time that that hole will produce before it heals itself over and sap stops flowing. So this healing was what caused our January taps to stop producing by early March, even though the weather was finally ideal at that point.

In future years, if I can't convince Bill to resist the urge to tap early, hopefully I'll at least convince him to try a test tree or maybe drill his holes just a little more shallow. That way we can re-drill the taps slightly deeper later in the season and regain pro-ductivity at that point. According to the tapping guidelines published by the University of Vermont Proctor Maple Research Center, a 1½-inch depth falls in the middle of the acceptable range for healthy trees, and it may be fine to drill as deep as 2 inches for your follow-up drilling. Of course, we need to keep in mind that under the right conditions, sap can move in all directions toward a small hole in the trunk, because it's flowing through tiny, 1-inch-long vessels in the tree that connect and flow in every direction, so deeper and wider will never give more sap. Deeper and wider will always cause more damage to the tree, so finding the ideal window of weather is much more productive than intentionally drilling deeper holes because we tapped too early to begin with.

3. What size tap do I use?

You may see $\frac{7}{16}$-inch taps in some places, but these are ones from a previous generation. Research has found that a $\frac{5}{16}$-inch tap will cause less damage to the tree, allow the tree to heal faster, and be just as efficient with sap yield.

4. Can I tap a tree that doesn't look so good?

If you tap a tree that isn't healthy, you'll cause more problems. If you noticed a tree had fewer leaves last summer, struggled with drought, suffered significant trunk damage, or fought insect problems, you should wait until it's healthy again, or at the very least install fewer taps in the stressed tree. Folks have done studies on this, and trees that were tapped under stress were much slower to heal (which leaves them open to more infection), quicker to suffer from branch dieback, and less likely to grow significant numbers of leaves the following spring.

5. What part of the sapwood should I tap into?

The most important factor to notice when you're placing taps is the quality of the wood that you're tapping into. No matter how perfectly you do everything else, you'll simply never have any quantity of sap if you're drilling into poor-quality wood. You want to tap into clear, white sapwood. To know if you've chosen a good quality sapwood, notice the color of your shavings. Light colored shavings indicate healthy sapwood. If the shavings are dark brown, that hole will be unproductive, so go ahead and drill another hole in a different location.

This is a great thing to keep in mind if you have some small or intermediate-sized trees you're tapping. If the tree is anything less than perfectly healthy, its growth rate may not sustain two taps. You'll know this after a few years of tapping because you'll tap into discolored, brown, non-white wood. If so, cut back to just one tap on that tree until it has had many years to grow larger. Once it has a larger diameter, its growth rate will overcome the annual damage of two taps, and light-colored shavings will testify to the fact.

As you place a tap, notice last year's tap location and stay at least 4 inches to the right or left of that hole, staggered up or down a little. On a younger tree, last year's hole may be difficult to find. Older trees, on the other hand, take longer to heal, so last year's tap location is easier to spot. If you do tap too close to last year's tap, you'll see darker wood shavings.

6. Which side of the tree should I tap?

Some sugarmakers have strong opinions about which side of the tree—the north-facing or the south-facing side—is most productive. In short, there is great short-term and long-term value in putting taps on both sides of your trees. For a link to a nice read that explains this in great detail, see the Resource Library on SoulyRested.com.

7. Should taps be installed at an angle?

To be sure you have a perfectly circular hole, and to avoid air leaks around your taps, you'll want to carefully drill a hole relatively straight into the tree, with a slightly upward angle to prevent sap pooling.

8. How deep should I place taps?

You'll want to keep your tap holes about 1½ inches deep. Going deeper causes greater damage to the tree without justifiable returns in quantity of sap. (Visit the Resource Library on SoulyRested.com if you'd like a detailed explanation.)

9. How many taps can I use in each tree?

Judge how many taps to install in a tree based on the tree's size. A tree 10–17 inches in diameter should only have 1 tap. You can insert two taps if the tree is 18–24 inches in

While some are adamant about tapping on only the north or south side of a tree (for different reasons), we like to vary the locations of our taps so that on any given day we tend to have a nice amount of sap.

diameter. And a tree over 25 inches in diameter can host 3 taps. While it is very tempting to over-tap a tree, research shows that each additional tap, regardless of the size or productivity of the tree, doesn't flow as well as the first tap. So it seems pointless to over-tap a tree, scar it more than necessary, and therefore limit your future productivity, when in reality you're not increasing your current output.

> *Decide how many taps to install in a tree based on its diameter.*
>
> | | |
> |---|---|
> | *10–17 inches* | *1 tap* |
> | *18–24 inches* | *2 taps* |
> | *25+ inches* | *3 taps* |

10. I have only a few trees. Should I even bother?

Syrup making requires stamina. To make a few cups of syrup, you'll need a 5-gallon bucket full of sap. So, yeah, show me a sugarmaker, and I'll show you a person with stamina.

You don't have to live in the Alaskan tundra or even have multiple acres of trees. Sometimes sugarmaking stamina isn't only about collecting a lot of sap. Sometimes stamina is about working hard to make syrup when you don't have any trees at all. Tyler Thompson embodies maple moxie. His resourcefulness earned him permission to tap 115 trees at the Camalachie Golf and Country Club near his home in Sarnia, Ontario. Virginia Laycock worked out a sweet deal with many of her neighbors who allow her to tap their trees in exchange for a jar of her syrup every year. Corinna West, on the other hand, has neighbors in Kansas City who are very happy to just see the process at work when she taps a tree or two in their yards. "I don't have any tree in my own yard that's good to tap, so I went around and talked to every neighbor who does." Last season, Corinna tapped 7 Norway maples, 5 silver maples, and 1 sycamore all around the neighborhood.

In general, you'll need five productive trees to wind up with a gallon of syrup at the end of a productive season. There are many variables, of course, and I didn't just make that up. That's according to numerous tests done by experts at places like the University of Vermont Proctor Maple Research Center. Most likely, if you have only one or two trees to tap, you won't harvest enough sap to make much syrup, but you'll love drinking your sap. Even if you're able to collect only a few cups worth of sap, it's a fantastic experience. Drinking ice cold water with a hint of sweetness (maple sap is 98 percent water, 2 percent sugar) that's been filtered by your tree is exhilarating, not to mention good for you.

Maple sap is bursting with antioxidants, minerals, enzymes, and phenolic compounds. In case you're an average person, like me, and you don't have the first clue what phenolic compounds are, I'll explain. They're compounds found in nature that have been shown to be, among other things, anti-inflammatory and even cancer-preventative. Now that's an impressive drink!

If you do want to try to boil down some sap and make syrup but you only have a few trees, you will need to save sap for many days to have enough to boil. Keep in mind that sap is sugar water, and it will grow bacteria very quickly if it gets even slightly warm. So be sure to keep your sap nice and cold until you're ready to boil it. If you plan on running it through a reverse osmosis filter (see page 68) do not do so until right before you boil your sap. Once it's been RO'd, the sugar concentration is at a high level that will quickly spoil.

So you're ready to tap?

Here's what you need to do:

- Choose a location that is 36 inches above ground and drill your tap hole, if this is your first time tapping the tree.

- If you've tapped the tree previously, locate last year's tap hole. White sapwood will have started to close in the tap hole, but it is usually still easy to find. Then move at least 4 inches to the right or left, and go slightly up, away from last year's hole, to choose this year's spot. (Once you choose which direction, continue in that direction in subsequent years.) You want to go 4 inches away because last year's tap has dead cells around it that will not conduct sap, so you want to tap into healthy cells. You will also want to move a few inches upward in your placement, so that you don't eventually girdle the tree over time.

- Remove any loose bark or moss on the tap site before you drill. This will help keep the drilled hole free of debris.

- Take your bit in and directly out, in one smooth motion when you drill. Going in and out multiple times causes additional, unnecessary damage. Go about 1½ inches

A thermos of hot water makes it super easy to fit in difficult connectors.

deep. Feel free to wrap a piece of tape around the drill bit to use as a guide. (Bill likes to cut a piece of tubing to slide over his bit that leaves 1½ inches of the bit exposed, so he can assure every tap is the same depth.)

- Avoid your natural impulse to blow into the hole you've just made to remove excess shavings or moss. In fact, blowing into the tap hole introduces bacteria from your mouth to the new tree wound. If there is loose material you want to remove from the tap hole, carry a small piece of stiff wire to use for this purpose.

- Use wrist strength, not arm strength, and a lightweight 8-ounce hammer, not a heavy hammer, to install your tap into the hole that you've just drilled. This will help you avoid splitting the wood around the tap. Hammer the tap in until you hear a change in pitch, letting you know the tap is secure. (If you continue to hammer at that point, you may crack the sapwood above and below your tap.) If the sap is flowing, you will immediately see sap dripping.

- Hook up tubing that leads to a bucket or collection tank, or hang a bucket or collection bag on the tree, and you're one step closer to delicious syrup!

- Carry a thermos of hot water while you're tapping if you struggle with getting tubing connectors to fit inside the tubing. Simply warm up the tubing by sticking it in the hot water before pushing your connectors in. They'll slide in easily, and the tubing will fit snugly around the connectors as it cools.

Save money

When the morning sun peeks her head over the horizon—bursting with streaks of soothing purples and vibrant pinks—I sometimes have a glimpse into the promise the day holds. If it's a really good morning I may even get to enjoy a maple scone or maple oatmeal with my tea. Sugar season often offers such mornings. I'll stoke the fire before letting Bixby out to romp in a fresh coating of snow, and I'll let out a satisfied sigh at the jars filled with deep amber liquid from last night's efforts.

When our maple syrup operation manager (aka Bill) spent less money for propane for sugarmaking in our second year, I splurged on a box of fancy jars for him to use, along with our mason jars. Why the splurge? It wasn't so much to make my awesome husband feel professional, but mainly to conserve our liquid gold. You see, once Bill had gotten

Morning offers a glimpse into the depth of promise that the day holds and, of course, the best mornings include maple.

his operation running smoothly and productively, he started giving away syrup to friends and family. The new jars would allow him to look generous without giving away so much of what he had worked so hard for.

The best part of this whole chapter might be the insight into how we spent much less money in our DIY maple syrup operation our second year than our first. Yep, on page 68 I'll explain how you too can save hundreds of dollars every year.

Professional looking jars can allow backyard sugarmakers to look quite generous, while giving away less of their product.

What if you're new to this?

If you're just starting out on this adventure, feel free to take it slow and easy. Don't worry about investing much money into your operation until you've tried it out and made sure this is really something you want to invest your time and effort into. In fact, I'd recommend just trying to make a few jars your first winter, by tapping just a handful of trees. Filter excess water out of your sap the old-fashioned—albeit a lot less scientific—way. Simply throw away ice that forms in your collection buckets. It's a natural way to filter out the water.

Get a feel for the fickleness of the process and the huge time commitment it is. Get a hands-on understanding of the fact that you can't plan for sap collection on your calendar; it has to be at the mercy of the weather forecast. You may experience 2 or 3 weeks with temperatures that are too cold for sap to run, then multiple days in a row—unexpectedly, overnight—of dozens of gallons of sap a day, every day, when daytime temps suddenly rise above 40°F.

I'm always happy to toss the ring of ice I find in my buckets from time to time, because that means my sap will have a higher sugar concentration.

Why so much boiling?

When the temperatures are perfect for causing tension in the trees, the sap flows with passion. We tapped a few dozen trees our second year. On our best day of that second season, our taps presented us with 30 gallons of sap in less than 24 hours.

Once 30 gallons of sap is boiled down, it equals 5–6 pint-sized jars of maple syrup. Yep, a 5-gallon bucket of sugar maple sap equals 2 cups of maple syrup. That means that most families would need 5-10 gallons of sap for enough syrup for just one pancake breakfast!

Needless to say, that means you have to spend a lot of time boiling down the sap, to take out the water.

A tree this size should have one tap, not two. Read on page 55 about why two taps won't produce more sap from this tree.

What could go wrong?

Sadly, while I've made lots of mistakes at this homesteading "thing," I must confess I've made the worst DIY maple syrup blunder of all. I walked away from a boiling pot when it needed my close attention. I got sidetracked with farm chores one evening and left the pot of boiling sap unattended when it was almost time for me to bring it in to the kitchen for the final, careful boil (more about this in the next chapter). You see, for the first long hours of boil, you can just periodically check on your pot of sap, adding more when appropriate, but when you're close to having just the right ratio of sugar to water, then you can't turn your back on it. Not only does the volume tell you it's close to time, but the warmer color—instead of the clear liquid you started with—announces this as well. You can't help but notice that amazing smell, too.

Yet there is a good side to the required constant boiling and monitoring: the pot provides a nice place to congregate and talk and, of course, taste the sweet sap. I've decided

A reverse osmosis filter will pay for itself in no time. See page 68 for more details.

SWEET SUGGESTIONS FROM A SUGARMAKER

Lou Plante remembers riding around to all the maples in his childhood neighborhood and emptying the sap buckets into the drums on the back of his dad's truck. They didn't sell a lot of syrup then, unlike today, which sees the family shipping out 500 gallons a year. In their new sugarhouse, nestled in the woods of New Hampshire, the Plante family is devoted to making their syrup as delicious as they can, the way it's been made for centuries—over a wood fire and without modern RO technology. When you taste their wood-fired syrup, you taste the character.

Lou Plante (right), with his brother and dad, are the three men behind their family's maple success.

Lou's advice?
"Don't be hard on yourself. The season's long enough that you have time to screw up and still get it right."

Lou's equipment recommendation?
Start with a turkey fryer, and order a grading kit for fun, then dive in and enjoy.

Lou's favorite recipe?

Mom's Extra-Easy Maple Cake
This is one of Lou's favorite childhood memories.
1. Pour half an inch to an inch of syrup in the bottom of an ungreased baking dish.
2. Pour a prepared vanilla cake mix on top. Bake according to box directions.

   When you remove the cake from the pan, you'll have a wonderful maple topping—on quite possibly the most amazing "box" cake you've ever had.

that I can justify doing this quite often, under the pretense that I have to know if it's almost ready.

DIY maple syrup making is not for the faint of heart or busy of schedule. DIY maple syrup making is also not for the poor of pocketbook. During our first winter we spent hundreds on propane alone. In the end, we made a grand total of eight (yes, eight) exorbitantly expensive pint-size jars of syrup.

Needless to say, our second year we knew we needed to find a way to save money and use less propane. Our solution cost us a few hundred dollars to build, but it paid for itself in the first year.

How can you save money while making maple syrup?

Bill, who loves a good excuse to build any cool contraption, built a reverse osmosis (RO) filter system that we run our sap through before boiling. The amazing beauty of this system is that it reduces our pre-boiling sap volume to half the amount we had before filtering. That means our boiling time is cut in half. That means our propane expense is cut in half. That means the maple syrup operation bookkeeper (aka me) is doubly happy.

The way the system works is pretty ingenious. It uses filters to pull out the "impurities" in the sap. It uses the same kind of filters homeowners buy for filtered water under a kitchen sink, only the homeowner discards the "impurities" and drinks the pure water. The sugarmaker, on the other hand, saves every ounce of those "impurities"—the sugars that make the syrup—and discards the pure water.

If you run your sap through a reverse osmosis system, keep in mind that you are creating sap with a much higher sugar concentration than before. Sap that has been filtered through an RO set up needs to be boiled right away. If you allow it to sit for too long before processing it will spoil quickly.

In the picture on page 66, one bucket holds the sap, and another is the filtered sap that we'll be boiling into syrup. The middle bucket holds the byproduct of reverse osmosis, which is called the permeate. Permeate is pure, crystal clear water that has come right out of the ground through a maple tree. It's a wonderful tasting, refreshing water that I enjoy drinking when Bill is running the filter system in the evenings. Did you know that people dish out more than $5 a bottle for this stuff? A brother/

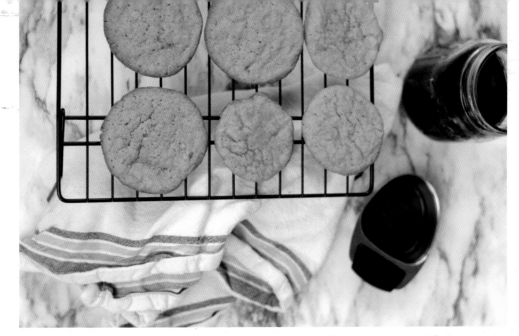

While syrup that has run through a reverse osmosis system costs less to make, our family doesn't find any reduction in flavor, either on our pancakes or in our maple cookies.

sister duo in Quebec have figured out a way to make a business based on this syrup-making byproduct, and they seem to be doing pretty well.

So an RO system not only will save you hundreds of dollars, but will also provide you with delicious syrup and pure, valuable permeate. Don't just take my word for it. The University of Vermont Proctor Maple Research Center has done extensive tests and published a report that goes into great detail about RO filters and if they're a good thing. To boil it all down for you, tests have shown no change in nutritional quality or taste of the end product if the sap was or was not run through an RO filter. Basically, it's filtering out all the good stuff, which you then can boil into syrup in half the amount of time. If you'd like directions to build your own reverse osmosis system, see the Resources section.

BILL'S TIP ON TAP

Does reverse osmosis change anything (taste, consistency, texture) about the final result?

tip

It saved us hundreds of dollars in fuel our second year, and none of us noticed anything different in the taste or consistency, but boy did we notice a difference in the bottom line. Michelle's always using maple syrup in a recipe, and RO'd syrup is just as delicious. Bonus, she's more eager to bake cookies because it didn't cost as much to make it. Maple snickerdoodles (see page 105)? Well they're worth every minute it took to assemble that RO.

OVERNIGHT MAPLE OATMEAL

Let the oats sit overnight, to soak up the maple goodness, and there aren't too many things yummier to wake up to. For ease of overnight storage, we love using mason jars. We layer the ingredients in the jars the night before we want to indulge in this warm goodness for breakfast.

2 cups rolled oats
1 teaspoon vanilla
2 cups milk
3 tablespoons brown sugar
¾ teaspoon cinnamon
3 tablespoons maple syrup

1. Using two pint-sized Mason jars, place half of the oats, vanilla, and milk in each jar. Shake or stir to mix well.

2. Combine brown sugar, cinnamon, and syrup and pour half into each of the jars. Shake or stir again.

3. Refrigerate the jars for at least two hours, but preferably overnight.

4. In the morning, microwave your maple-infused oats for a few minutes, right in the mason jar, stir, and enjoy warm, wholesome goodness with no effort. Let's face it, some mornings, we need no effort, am I right?

YIELDS TWO SERVINGS

Lazy Girl's maple sugar

If you're craving maple sugar on your oatmeal but don't want to dirty a pan and mixer, you can try this alternative. In a small bowl, stir together sugar and maple syrup. For every ¼ cup of sugar, add 1 teaspoon maple syrup. That's it. It's coarser and not nearly as yummy as the real stuff, but it definitely works in a pinch.

OATMEAL CHOCOLATE CHIP SKILLET CAKE

When Kayla whipped this up one spring afternoon, I wasn't too excited. I'm an icing kind of girl. If I'm eating a dessert without icing, it better be chocolate—but when your teen daughter creates something in the kitchen—in cast iron nonetheless—you take a piece with a smile. Turned out my smile was genuine after the first taste.

½ cup butter

¼ cup shortening

2 eggs

¾ cup maple syrup

¼ tsp almond extract

2 teaspoon vanilla

1¼ cups flour

1 cup oats

1 teaspoon baking soda

1½ cups chocolate chips

> **If it can't be maple, I still make it unrefined.**
> *Throughout this book wherever "sugar" or "brown sugar" is mentioned in a recipe, I use whole cane sugar or brown whole cane sugar. All-natural, unprocessed maple products will always be my favorite, but if I need to use a more traditional option, I prefer a whole cane sugar to a refined one. It's less processed, retains a little of the natural cane syrup, and offers a better taste than refined sugar.*

1. Preheat the oven to 350°F.

2. Lightly grease a 10- or 12-inch oven-safe skillet with butter. (A 10-inch skillet will give you a thicker cake, of course. I always grab my cast iron for this recipe.)

3. In a large mixing bowl, beat the butter and shortening until light and fluffy. Add the eggs, one at a time, until combined. Slowly add in the maple syrup, almond extract, and vanilla, beating until combined. Add the flour, oats, and baking soda, and mix until fully incorporated.

4. Stir in the chocolate chips, and spread the batter out in the prepared skillet. Place the skillet in the oven and bake for 20–22 minutes. (It's okay if the center comes out a little gooey.) Remove from the oven and let cool for 3–5 minutes, then dig in— preferably with a generous scoop of homemade ice cream.

YIELDS ONE 10–12-INCH CAKE OR 8 SERVINGS

THE BEST-EVER MAPLE SCONES

I'm going to be totally honest. I never even considered including a scone recipe in this book. Because (here comes the brutally honest part) I don't like scones. Then Kayla made these one day when she was looking for something to do with her extra cream from the previous day's milking, and I had to make an exception. Their velvety sweetness and moist cakey-ness make them a perfect choice for breakfast on a chilly fall morning. Who am I kidding? These babies are perfect for any occasion, any time.

4½ cups flour

½ cup brown sugar

2 tablespoons baking powder

½ teaspoon salt

1½ teaspoon cinnamon

pinch of nutmeg

1 cup butter, cold and cubed

¼ cup + 2 tablespoons maple syrup

2 eggs

1 cup cream

1 teaspoon vanilla extract

For maple glaze:

1½ –2 cups powdered sugar

3–4 tablespoons heavy cream

2 tablespoons maple syrup

½ teaspoon vanilla extract

1. Preheat oven to 400°F.

2. Mix flour, brown sugar, baking powder, salt, cinnamon, and nutmeg together in a large bowl, then cut butter in with a fork (or just work it in with your fingers) until the dough resembles coarse crumbs.

3. Add in rest of ingredients, stirring just until combined. Turn out the crumbly dough onto a floured surface, working it until it comes together. Make 2 balls with the dough, patting each down into a 1-inch-thick circle. Slice each circle into 8 triangular pieces.

4. Place the scones onto baking sheets and bake for 15–16 minutes, or until the scones turn light brown on the edges.

5. Mix glaze ingredients, adding more cream if you would like the glaze thinner and more powdered sugar if you would like the glaze thicker. Drizzle the icing over the scones if you're like my daughter who goes for aesthetics, or like me and dip the tops right into the glaze.

YIELDS 16 MEDIUM-SIZED SCONES

GIANT CANDY COOKIE

I'll admit it: When I walk by the grocery store bakery and eye those giant cookies covered in icing, I always want one, but I never buy it. I'd like to say it's because I never buy store-bought baked goods (yeah, right) or because my family eats only healthy, fresh fruit for dessert (yeah, right again), but no, I don't buy one because they're so expensive! So I figured out how to make them myself. I forgo the icing and refined sugar, but not the candy-coated chocolate pieces 'cause a girl needs chocolate now and then.

¾ **cup butter**

¼ **cup maple sugar**

1 extra-large egg

⅔ **cup maple syrup**

1 tsp vanilla

2 cups flour

¾ **tsp baking soda**

¾ **cup semi-sweet chocolate chips**

½ **cup candy-coated chocolate pieces**

1. Preheat oven to 350°F.
2. Cream room-temperature butter in a mixer with the maple sugar. Add the egg and cream well again. Mix in maple syrup and vanilla. Mix flour and baking soda and add to the mixer slowly until well incorporated. Mix in chips and candy-coated chocolate pieces
3. Spread dough out in a 14-inch cast iron pizza pan and bake for 25 minutes. Feel free to serve it warm with ice cream on top, or slice it up into cookies bars and they will store nicely for many days.

YIELDS ONE COOKIE. WELL, ONE COOKIE THAT FEEDS AN ARMY.

Boil Well

MAKE AMBER, AMBROSIAL SYRUP, ONE SWEET STEP AT A TIME

Many years' worth of failures have taught me a lot about backyard maple syrup making. In fact, I'm sure I'll still be learning decades from now. After all, I've been a wife for a quarter of a century and mom for 23 years, and I'm still learning from my failures in both of those endeavors. By God's grace, my marriage is solid, my daughters are amazing young women, and my maple syrup is goldenly delicious, despite my ineptitude in all three areas. This chapter will walk you step-by-step through the process my family goes through daily, every sugar season, to make maple syrup.

Step 1: Gather the sap

Kayla, Hayley, and I try to gather all the sap from the buckets each day before the maple syrup operations manager arrives on scene (i.e., before Bill gets home from a long day of fixing cars, or "wrenching" as he would say). So by 4 pm we bundle up and head out. We usually split up to inspect a section of tapped trees. On our best days, all the 5-gallon containers at the base of each tree are beautifully full. It's a lot of work carting them all back to the house, and it gets harder every year as we expand the circumference of our taps, but I enjoy the good excuse to get outside and enjoy profitable exercise after a long, cold winter's day. Back at the house, we line up our 5-gallon buckets, all ready for processing.

When Bill gets home, it's usually he, Kayla, and I who walk up "the back" to empty out the 75-gallon drum that all of our sap lines feed into. And Bixby. Bixby is always a given.

Since the drum is in the heart of the woods, it's much colder than the small buckets that are situated near our house, where they're warmed by the afternoon sun. In fact, until spring temperatures start rising a little (last year this wasn't until the first week of April), the sap in the drum is often frozen by evening. If this is the case and the sap is running well, I'll make sure we empty the drum during the afternoon, before it freezes. To empty our big drum, we use a handy dandy battery-operated pump that enables us to draw the sap out of the 75-gallon container and into buckets that we can carry back to the house.

Our dream is to one day have a tractor that we can use for collecting the sap daily. For now, thoughts of maple-infused cookies in the oven always make the hard work go a little faster. Until we can actually attain a luxurious tractor, we'll be building up our biceps (and, thankfully, walking off some of those evening cookie calories).

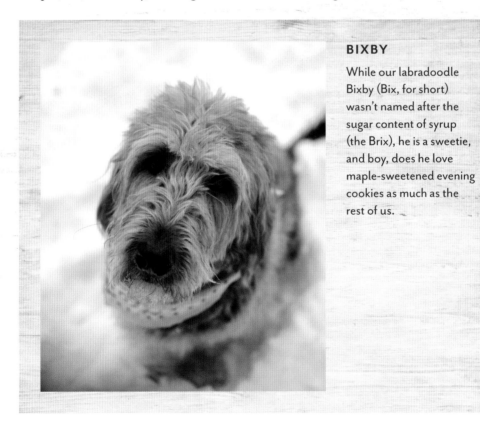

BIXBY

While our labradoodle Bixby (Bix, for short) wasn't named after the sugar content of syrup (the Brix), he is a sweetie, and boy, does he love maple-sweetened evening cookies as much as the rest of us.

MAPLE BUTTER DOG BONES

Need a special gift for a dog-loving friend? Mix a batch of these for her coddled canine and a batch of any of the maple-infused cookies on pages 102–109, place some in a basket with a jar of maple syrup, and you'll present her with the sweetest dog-owner gift ever.

⅓ cup maple syrup
3 tablespoons water
3 tablespoons Maple Peanut Butter (see page 202)
1¼ cups flour

1.   Preheat oven to 325°F.

2.   Mix all ingredients together well. Once it's nice and crumbly, simply work the dough with your hands to get a nice consistency.

3.   Roll dough out, press with an embossing rolling pin (if you like), cut into shapes, and bake for 20–40 minutes, depending on the size and thickness of treats, as well as how soft or hard your dog likes them. Ones that are baked hard will last for several months in a sealed container. Soft ones should probably be refrigerated if your pooch doesn't eat them all in a few days!

YIELDS 20–24 3-INCH DOG BONES

BILL'S TIP ON TAP

Should I keep the ice that forms in my buckets?

No. The sugar content will not freeze as quickly as water, so I'm always pleased when I remove a lid and find a big ring of ice has formed all around the wall of the bucket. I toss the ice and spend less time and fuel in boiling down the sap. Yes, there may be traces of sugar in that ice, but the percentage is too low to justify the cost of boiling it.

Step 2: Filter the sap, the old-fashioned way

Before doing anything at all with the buckets full of sap, we filter it. We set up a reusable felt cone filter and pour it all through. The options here are numerous.

Step 3: Filter the sap, the new-fangled way

The next thing we do is run the sap through our reverse osmosis (RO) filter (see page 68). While this is not a necessary step—you certainly can make wonderful syrup without an RO—I can't imagine sugarmaking without it. Our simple, homemade

RO filter works wonderfully and saves us hundreds on propane costs every year, reducing the amount of sap we have to boil by half.

Step 4: Boil the sap outside

After the sap has run through the RO filter, we turn on the propane tank, set our giant 16-gallon pot on top of the flame, and fill the pot ¾ full of the filtered sap. We never fill it more than that because sap has a natural tendency to boil up and over a pan's edge when no one is looking.

We add more sap often, always keeping it at the ¾-full mark or less. On the really productive days, when we gathered lots of sap, we can't finish it all in one night. While we try not to RO more than we can boil, we'll label the filtered sap buckets "RO," with tape on their lids, so we don't mix them up the next day with straight sap that we've collected, although, honestly, we'd have to be half asleep to mix them up. The filtered sap is golden tinted; straight sap looks like water. We also make sure never to let RO'd sap sit any longer than absolutely necessary. With such a high sugar content, it'll spoil quickly.

Step 5: Filter the old-fashioned way, again

Then, we filter again. Nope, no one said anything worth eating was easy. When the outside pot has boiled down to only a few inches of beautiful amber-colored sap, it's time to bring it inside. When it's getting close to that point, it's important to never leave it unattended. It takes just a few minutes of distraction for the sap to boil down to burnt-on, burnt-up mess. I've learned this the hard way, the got-to-go-out-and-buy-a-new-pot-tomorrow way.

Once you take it off the outside heat source, you'll need to filter the boiled-down sap to get out impurities that blew in while you boiled. If you don't get the debris out, your syrup will taste bitter.

Backyard sugarmakers often burn the midnight propane to get the day's sap done and bottled.

We started off our first year using coffee filters to do this step, but it was pretty much pointless, because coffee filters leave lots of sediment. Now we use a reusable, washable cone filter. We actually have quite a few of these. It's the same kind we use in step 2. We originally just made a makeshift holder for it out of a heavy-duty hanger, which worked fine. You can buy a filter stand, if you'd like to look like you know what you're doing.

We pour our syrup from our turkey fryer pot into our kitchen pot through a filter. Even when it's makeshift, it does a nice job of removing the debris that has blown into the syrup while it was boiling outside.

Step 6: Boil the sap inside

Up to this point you want to do all your boiling outside to keep the sticky sap steam off of your kitchen walls, but once you're getting close to syrup consistency, you need to monitor the boil closely inside. There will still be some sticky steam, so our maple syrup operations manager designed and installed a fancy steam tunnel to direct steam out our downdraft vent. In other words, Bill rigged an impromptu temporary set up with chimney pipe pieces he had sitting around, and it's been in use every year since. The makeshift extension to our downdraft vent may look a little odd, but it keeps sticky steam off our kitchen walls, so it's a "win."

Our makeshift vent works well, so it's a multiyear "impromptu" solution to sticky walls.

One evening last winter, when we were boiling on the kitchen stove, we weren't watching every single second. That was a messy mistake, because, like I said, when sap boils over, it does so very rapidly and with great enthusiasm. Sadly, we didn't learn the first time. After 20 minutes of sticky clean up, we put the pot back on the heat and–I'm embarrassed to admit this–walked away for a minute. I can proudly say we did not make that same mistake a third time that night. Because we packed it up in utter discouragement and went to bed.

When all is going well, we get the filtered sap up to a boil of exactly 219°F. This perfect temperature does depend on your altitude; you need the sap boiling at exactly 7°F above the boiling point of water. At that temperature a magic thing happens. Sap becomes syrup. Just like that. The plain-old-step-sister-like tree sap becomes the Cinderella of syrup. Except it does take a lot more than just waving a magic wand.

Ideally, at 219°F you should test your syrup's sugar content with one of the gadgets explained on pages 91–93. Your sugar content should be at 66 percent. If it's under that perfect measurement, you would let it boil another minute or so and test it again. If you're just starting out in this sugarmaking adventure and don't want to invest in extra gadgets yet, you can make do with just a thermometer. Most people agree that backyard sugarmakers will do just fine if they have a good thermometer and know how to use it, especially with the aid of some apps and websites I mention on page 94. While I like to have several thermometers on hand, you only truly need one. No matter how high-tech your thermometer is, if you want accurate measurements, you will need to calibrate it every time you're boiling down sap. Don't worry, it's not as difficult as it sounds.

When I first heard someone say I needed to calibrate my thermometer, I pictured Bill taking it into his shop for a "tune up." (He's just a sugarmaker on the side, and an amazing mechanic by day.) I pictured him hooking our thermometer up to a special machine and running some diagnostics on it. I have no idea why this was my first thought, except I guess I associated calibration with car engine tune ups.

The good news is that it's way easier than that. You just need to get a pot of boiling water, place your thermometer in the water, and notice what it registers. While you probably already know that, in general, water boils at 212°F, you may not know that it varies slightly from day to day, and it also depends on other factors, like your elevation. (I didn't know this before I started making syrup, but then again I also thought I needed a mechanic to calibrate my thermometer!)

If you want accurate measurements, you will need to calibrate your thermometer every time you're boiling down sap.

Syrup boiled to too high of a Brix will offer you some delicious rock candy in the bottom of your jars.

So whatever your thermometer reads when the water is boiling is your boiling point for the day (and for your specific thermometer, which of course might also be "off" a little). You then add 7 degrees to that number, and you have the perfect, magic number for making syrup on that given moment, of that given day, with that given thermometer, in your given location (I know that's a lot of givens). Even better, use one of the apps on page 94 to find out the perfect number of degrees over boiling you're looking for on that exact day. I kid you not, this too varies every day. Serious sugarmakers are pretty much weathermen on the side.

If you're feeling a little lazy (we all do now and then), or if you're just feeling really sure of yourself (yep, sadly, we all do that too often, no?), then you can just go with the magic number of 219°F and you'll be pretty close.

How do you achieve the Goldilocks of syrup? You know, the syrup that's not too this or too that, but just right? The right thickness and the right amount of sugar require a measurement. In the syrup world, it's called "Brix." The perfect amount of sugar is 66–68 percent Brix. Syrup perfection exists only in that little window: not too runny, which would really just be thick, yummy maple water, and not too thick, which means it will start forming crystals, growing maple rock candy in the bottom of your jars. So how do you measure this evasive "Brix?" That's a question that will get you five different answers if you ask five different sugarmakers. These are the tools that will help you have perfectly boiled syrup. Which should you use? That's the $20,000 question.

Syrup hydrometer

Some sugarmakers will tell you that a syrup hydrometer is a tool that will guarantee perfect syrup every time. I'm here to tell you if a sugarmaker tells you anything guarantees perfect syrup they're lying. On the other hand, if you want a tool that will help you reach syrup perfection most of the time, a hydrometer is one good option. It works on the principle that you'll know the amount of sugar in a sweet liquid if you measure the density of the liquid. When you're making syrup all that really matters is how much sugar is in the sap. You spend a long time boiling away the water in the sap so you can taste that wonderful sugar, so you want to be sure to get the perfect amount.

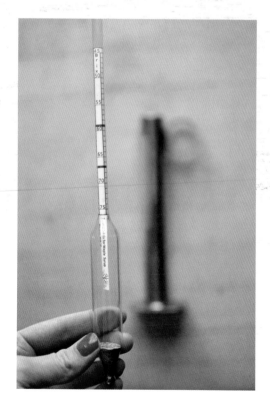

The sugar is measured on most hydrometers by using a scale of degrees Brix (shown on the hydrometer as °Bx). One °Bx equals 1 percent sugar content. At the risk of making this sound more complicated than it is, maybe I should explain that hydrometers have two scales. The other one, other than Brix, is Baume, and 66° Brix is equivalent to 35.6° Baume. Most hydrometers mark the perfect level with an easy-to-see red line.

To use your hydrometer, fill the tall metal cup, which you have to purchase separately from your hydrometer, with the syrup that you're finishing off. Place a bowl or large plate under your cup, so you can collect the overflow, and then gently place your hydrometer in the filled cup. It will float. The hydrometer, by the way, looks like a giant, old-fashioned thermometer like Mom used to place under your tongue when you didn't feel so hot. Like Mom's ancient tool, a hydrometer is made of glass. When it finishes bobbing in the syrup, you can read the measurement on the hydrometer at the top line of your syrup. If the red line is even with the surface of your syrup in the cup, you're ready to bottle. Pour the cup full of syrup back in your pan, and start filtering and bottling.

If your Brix reading is too low, and the red line floats below the surface of the syrup, you need to keep boiling your sap and try measuring it again in a little while. If, on the other hand, your Brix reading is too high, and the red line floats above the surface, your syrup is too dense with sugar. While that may sound extra yummy, it makes overly thick syrup with giant crystals that grow from the bottom of the jar as the syrup cools. No need to worry if your hydrometer sinks too low. Just mix in a little partially-boiled sap, cook the syrup a little bit longer and retest it.

Tips for using a hydrometer

- Purchase one specifically for syrup making. Others may be calibrated for beer and wine making.

- Place it in hot water to warm it before using it. Otherwise putting it right into 219°F syrup may crack the glass.

- Wash it well after every single use. It will give an inaccurate reading if it's covered in sticky residue.

- Keep in mind that you will need to purchase a separate sap hydrometer if you want to measure the sugar content of your sap, right out of the tree.

Refractometer

If you want to go a little-fancier but a whole-lot-easier route, you could consider a refractometer. It's a neat tool, and it does exactly what its name insinuates. It measures how light is refracted through your sugary, boiled down sap, as well as your sap right out of the tree.

Place some sap or syrup in a little cup at the end of the manual option and hold it up to the light. If you go with the even fancier digital version, you just place a drop of syrup in and push a button. As light reflects through your syrup, it's refracted, and this tool measures it, on a Brix scale.

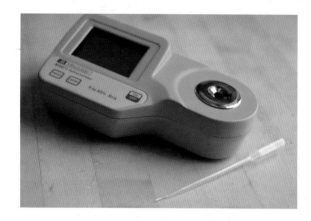

You do have a choice of manual or digital refractometers, but make sure the one you pick offers Automatic Temperature Compensation (or ATC). Then you won't have to use a thermometer and a conversion table to compensate for the sap temperature. Refractometers are more versatile–they can measure the sugar content in your sap, as well as your syrup. With hydrometers, you'll need two different instruments to accomplish the work of one refractomer. Of course, neither of them can make your pancakes for you.

Murphy compensation cup

This tool includes a gauge on the cup. You need to fill the cup with syrup, float a hydrometer in the syrup—as described on the previous page—and read the dial. The dial notes what your hydrometer needs to read, based on whatever temperature the syrup is in the cup. If the dial matches the reading on your hydrometer, your syrup is good to go.

Step 7: Filter the old-fashioned way, one last time

After you've invested many long hours, it's finally almost time to bottle your liquid gold. Don't skip this one last opportunity to filter the syrup. Whenever you pull a new jar out of your pantry or decide to gift a jar to a very special friend or family member, you'll be glad you filtered one last time. Trust me.

Now I won't pretend that this last filtering is easy. It's anything but. In fact, this is one of the most common topics you'll find on social media involving maple syrup making. The filters get clogged easily, and the syrup cools rapidly, and you are left with this cold, thick syrup backed up in your filter. If you decide to throw in the towel and just pour your unfiltered syrup into bottles, I guarantee you within a few hours you'll notice the minerals (known by sugarmakers as the dreaded "niter" or "sugar sand") settling on the bottom of your jars. During the sugaring season of 2018, I had sugarmakers from across the country—pros as well as backyard newbies—all telling me it was a really rough year for niter. No one seems to know exactly why some years are drastically worse than others, but it all comes down to the mineral components of the sap. I assume certain weather conditions have an impact. As sap is heated up and concentrated into syrup, some of the minerals that occur naturally in sap separate from the overall sap "solution" and we see those minerals in the syrup. If we don't

> *If you find yourself stuck with a lot of niter in the bottom of your jars of syrup, there's no need to waste it. Let it set for a month or two until the niter has fully settled to the bottom, pour off your syrup, and use the calcium-rich, maple-flavored sugar sand in your baking, replacing sugar in a recipe in a 1:1 ratio with niter.*

filter extremely well, those minerals pile up in the bottom of our syrup jars and look like sand, thus the moniker "sugar sand."

In a desperate effort to get the syrup through the filter before it's too cool to bottle, we often would roll the long handles of wooden spoons down the sides of the filter bag, forcing the syrup through. Unfortunately we were also forcing all the sediment, or niter, right on through the filter too.

Filtering tips

- Skimming your sap while it's cooking outside will help avoid some of the buildup that clogs your filter.

- Using wool filters seems to be more effective than using synthetic ones.

- Lining your main filter with multiple prefilters allows you to pull prefilters out, one at a time, when the flow slows down.

- Wetting your filters in hot water (or hot sap) before filtering makes them more productive.

- Washing the reuseable filter with each use definitely helps, so we always have a few spares on hand.

- Spraying the filter with your sink spray nozzle, if you have one, is an effective way to wash it.

- Pushing the middle of the filter up (as seen in the picture on the following page), or using a special holder that arranges it that way, provides more contact area for filtering.

- Drying your filter by simply hanging it—never wringing it—makes a big difference. Wringing the filter can crush the fibers of the filter, and it will quickly be inefficient.

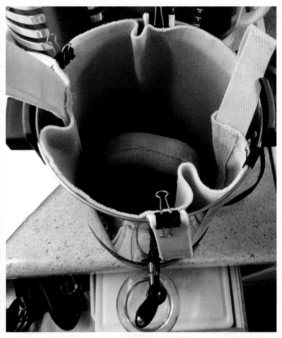

If you diligently remove foam as it builds up on your boiling sap, filtering will be easier.

Bryan Smagacz, a backyard sugarmaker, uses clips from an office supply store to hold his filter in place as he pours.

After years of clogged filters and cloudy syrup, Bill designed a sweet DIY filter press.

Since syrup shrinks a little as it cools, there's no need to leave head space in your jars.

- Purchasing a new filter every year helps too. We keep 3 on hand. The newest one gets used at that last, most crucial stage, right before bottling. Then last year's filter removes debris when we pour boiled down sap from our outside pot into our inside one, over the stove. Our oldest filter spends its third year of life as that initial, not-as-important filter, when we're pouring the sap into our boiling pot outside, where the whole process begins.

- Keeping syrup hot the entire time you're filtering is an ongoing challenge but important. Once it starts to cool down (which happens quickly), filtering comes to a halt. You'll need to reheat the unfiltered syrup, but be sure to keep it under 190°F, or you may create more niter to clog your filter. One great solution involves investing in an insulated coffee urn, which regulates the syrup temperature and gives you a convenient spout to bottle from. Another solution is a DIY filter press—built with two 12-quart pots and a portable air tank—that mimics a professional filter press, at a tiny fraction of the cost. See the Resources section for more information.

Step 8: Bottle the syrup

The first thing I do when I bring the boiling sap in for the final boil inside is to place canning lids into a little pot of simmering water on the stove, so they're ready to seal when our jars are ready. We use a canning funnel to make it easier to pour the hot syrup into each jar, and as we pour, we fill each jar as close to the top as we can without spilling. There's no need for head space, because syrup shrinks a

> **MICHELLE'S TIP ON TAP**
> **How long will maple syrup keep?**
>
> *Once you open a jar of maple syrup, you will need to refrigerate it, because it is an all-natural product with no preservatives. According to the Massachusetts Maple Producers Association, unopened maple syrup will keep indefinitely.*

> **MICHELLE'S TIP ON TAP**
> **Do I need to water bath can my homemade syrup?**
>
> *Because I love it when something that seems pretty complicated is made a little more "simple," I love the answer to this question: a big, whole-hearted, unequivocal "No." Water bath canning is not only not necessary; it is counterproductive. If you reheat your syrup in a water bath, more niter could form, and nobody wants that.*

little as it cools. Using a magnetic canning lid lifter, we remove lids from the pan of hot water and screw them onto each jar, immediately after filling it with syrup. At this point, if you'd like, you can invert the jars, if you're using canning jars, to make it extra easy for the lids to seal. With any jar it's also fine to simply lay each one on its side for a few seconds so the hot syrup can fill any head space and sanitize the whole jar. With the fancy syrup jars I recently purchased, there's no need to boil lids. We just screw them on as soon as we fill the jars as they're self-sealing. For those I simply lay them on their side for a few seconds after screwing the lids on.

It is important to make sure you sanitize and seal your jars correctly, even though, according to the University of Maine Coop Extension, harmful bacteria like E. coli and salmonella cannot survive in maple syrup (Crazy enough, maple syrup is too high in sugar content for those creepy bacteria to be happy. Go figure.), but yeasts and molds, not unlike me, enjoy sugar. So they can—and will—grow in maple syrup if we don't finish and package it correctly.

We have to boil the sap to different temperatures and follow different steps if we're making maple sugar or—my favorite—deliciously creamy maple cream. (I give you the complete low down on how to make those two heavenly delicacies in chapter 7.) Great news—you don't even have to tap one tree before you can enjoy making those treats. You can make them from maple syrup you purchase from a great sugarhouse online! Really. I wouldn't lie about something so all-naturally tasty.

Bottling tips

- Clean your containers in warm water. If you use soap, make sure to rinse them thoroughly. We run ours through the dishwasher before filling them. You don't need to go overboard as the hot syrup will sanitize the jars.

- Watch the temperature. Never bottle if the syrup is cooler than 180°F. If some does cool before you have it all bottled, simply reheat it. But keep the temperature below 190° or you'll need to refilter, since niter will often form at that temperature.

- Fill your jars to the top. No need for head space because syrup shrinks when it cools.

- Lay each jar on its side for a few seconds after you close it, and the hot syrup will sanitize any head space you may have left. If you're using canning jars, you can even set them upside down.

- Separate your jars or bottles with plenty of space around them as they cool. If you line them up close together while they're hot, the syrup will continue to caramelize in the containers and may get excessively dark. On the other hand, if you're bottling tiny jars (smaller than 8 ounces), they'll cool quickly. To make sure there's enough heat to kill any germs, keep those little guys close together and covered with a towel.

MAPLE CHOCOLATE CHIP COOKIES

Having to chill the dough makes for a more finicky cookie recipe than I typically like to deal with, but their subtle maple taste and perfect texture make these cookies worth the effort.

1 cup butter, at room temperature

1½ cups light brown sugar

½ cup white sugar

2 eggs, at room temperature

1½ teaspoon vanilla extract

¼ cup maple syrup

3¼– 3½ cups all-purpose flour

2 teaspoon cornstarch

1 teaspoon baking powder

1 teaspoon baking soda

1 teaspoon salt

2 cups chocolate chips

¼ cup chocolate chunks

1. In a large bowl, beat butter and sugars. Mix in eggs, vanilla, and maple syrup.

2. Combine 3¼ cups flour, cornstarch, baking powder, baking soda, and salt together in a separate bowl, then beat the flour mixture into the butter mixture.

3. Stir in chips and chocolate chunks.

4. Chill the dough for at least 30 minutes. Add the additional ¼ cup of flour only if the dough doesn't seem quite thick enough after refrigeration. (Before chilling, my dough is always too gooey, but I resist the urge to keep adding flour because I have made these cookies too cake-like by doing that in the past.)

5. Preheat oven to 325°F.

6. Place teaspoonfuls of dough a few inches apart on cookie sheets as they spread when they bake. Bake for 12–14 minutes, switching trays from top to bottom racks halfway through. (The cookies may appear a bit underdone, but their edges should just begin to turn golden brown.) Cool cookies completely on cookie sheets, where they'll flatten, and their centers will harden slightly. After they've cooled, they're chewy and moist.

Note: Keep the unbaked cookie dough in your fridge while you're waiting to put the next batch in the oven. Even a few minutes at room temperature makes the dough sticky and hard to work with.

YIELDS ABOUT 4 DOZEN COOKIES

For a delicious gluten-free alternative, substitute gluten-free, all-purpose flour, add ¾ teaspoon of xanthan gum, and take 2 minutes off the total baking time.

GINA'S MAPLE SNICKERDOODLES

She's a fan of the Baltimore Orioles and snickerdoodles. Yet while she's been my best friend since the 7th grade, Gina has never tried to convince me to switch my baseball allegiance or cookie preference. So when I came up with this out-of-the-ballpark-yummy maple syrup version of her favorite cookie, I had to name it after my bestie.

¾ cup butter, softened

¾ cup granulated sugar

¼ cup brown sugar

¼ cup pure maple syrup

2 teaspoon vanilla extract

1 egg

2 teaspoon baking soda

2¼ cups all-purpose flour

1½ teaspoon ground cinnamon

1 teaspoon cream of tartar

½ teaspoon salt

For the coating:

¼ cup maple sugar

1 tablespoon ground cinnamon

1. Cream the butter and sugars together, then beat in the maple syrup, vanilla, and egg.

2. Combine the rest of the ingredients together in a separate bowl, and slowly add them to the butter and egg mixture.

3. Then comes the hard part. You have to put the dough in the fridge and let it cool for an hour. When your hour wait is almost up, preheat your oven to 350°F and mix your sugar coating in a small bowl.

4. Roll the nicely chilled dough into about 1½-inch balls, and then roll each ball in cinnamon sugar coating. Place them 2 inches apart on the baking sheet, and bake for 8–10 minutes. You'll know you've reached snickerdoodle perfection when your tops have cracked slightly.

While I do occasionally make these cookies with zero refined sugar by substituting 1 cup of maple sugar for all of the white and brown sugars, they always bake into a more cake-like consistency. In fact, I don't call them snickerdoodles. When I use only maple sweeteners, I call them maple cinnamon cookies. Of course these cookies taste good, no matter what you call 'em.

YIELDS A FEW DOZEN COOKIES

OLD-FASHIONED BUTTER COOKIES

I'm astounded at just how much I love butter cookies, since they seem so, dare I say it, plain. Then one day my baking world was rocked. I discovered these amazing embossed rolling pins made of maple hardwood. (Ummmm, maple? Seriously.) I immediately envisioned a pie covered in a beautiful maple leaf pattern. I tracked down Lisa, the artisan who made these brilliant tools, and we hashed out ideas for a perfect design, which looks just as gorgeous on butter cookies. Suddenly butter cookies aren't plain anymore.

1 cup butter
¾ cup sugar
1 egg
2 tablespoons maple syrup

1½ teaspoons maple (or vanilla) extract
½ teaspoon salt
3 cups flour

1. Cream your butter and sugar together first. Then add the egg, maple syrup, and extract.

2. Mix salt into flour then blend into the rest of the mixture gradually. After it is well incorporated, divide your dough in 3 separate balls, wrap them in plastic wrap, and chill them for an hour in the fridge (or a shorter time in the freezer).

3. Preheat oven to 300°F.

4. After it's chilled, roll out one ball of dough, leaving it rather thick, so that after you've rolled over it one more time with the embossing roller, you have ¼-inch thick cookies.

5. Wrap up any extra pieces you have after cutting out your cookies and rechill while you do the same thing with another small ball of dough, until you've cut out all your cookies.

6. Place cookies on tray (no need to worry about spacing; these cookies don't puff up), and bake for 10–12 minutes, until the cookie bottoms start to turn a light brown.

YIELDS ABOUT 2 DOZEN SINGLE COOKIES OR A DOZEN SANDWICH COOKIES

It's doubly sweet to make sandwich cookies out of these buttery treats. Just whip up this cookie-cream filling: Mix 3½ cups powdered sugar, ½ tablespoon sugar (white or maple are both delicious), ½ teaspoon vanilla extract, ½ cup coconut oil, and 2 tablespoons hot water. Add additional hot water, one tablespoon at a time, if needed.

MAPLE CARAMEL COOKIES

This right here is one of my favorite cookies of all time. It's my celebratory cookie when my team makes it to the World Series, my "let my daughters know they're extra special" cookie, my "take to a neighbor who needs cheering up" cookie. Accompanied with a tall glass of cold milk, they make everything better.

1 cup butter, softened	**2½ cups flour**
1 cup dark brown sugar	**¾ cup cocoa**
2 egg yolks	**1 teaspoon baking soda**
⅔ cup maple syrup	**30 caramel-filled chocolate candies**
2 teaspoons vanilla	

1. Preheat oven to 350°F.
2. Beat butter and brown sugar together. Add egg yolks and beat well. Then mix in syrup and vanilla. Combine the flour, cocoa, and baking soda, then mix them in as well. I know recipes usually tell you to mix all those dry ingredients in a separate bowl, but I'm not big on having one more dirty bowl to wash, so I simply add them in one neat pile in my mixing bowl, then with a fork make sure the 3 ingredients are well mixed before turning on the beater.
3. Your dough will be a little sticky. Coating your fingers in a little flour or freezing your dough for a few minutes should be all you need to make it perfect to work with.
4. Mold a spoonful of dough around a caramel-filled chocolate candy and place cookies a few inches apart on ungreased sheets.
5. Bake for 7–10 minutes or until set. Cookies will still be gooey when you remove them from the oven, so make sure you let them sit and cool on the warm trays, which will make them the perfect consistency.

YIELDS 30 COOKIES

Bow Out

HOW A SUGARMAKER FACES THE BITTERSWEET
ARRIVAL OF SPRING

Almost as important as knowing when and how to start tapping maple trees, sugar-makers need to know when to stop tapping maple trees as well. During the weeks on the farm when we're finally putting away the last of the syrup-making supplies (it's a many-week process for us), we're flooded with the energetic, melodious signs of spring. Sap collection tools and buckets are washed, stacked, and dried. Chicks and ducklings are hatching under the care of sweet, broody hens and ducks. Baby robins are hatching under parents' watchful eyes under barn eaves and in nooks of poplar trees. The grass, so long covered in snow, comes alive in a green hue that, every year, always seems more vibrant than we can remember, and beautiful yellow blooms fill the sugar maples. While syrup season usually plows into us before we're ready most years, it seems to halt just as abruptly. Truth be told, the sud-denness might sadden us were it not for the joys of spring, and the wonderful feeling of getting back to work on the farm, that replace the sweetness of sap.

There are different factors that tell you it's time to stop your daily collec-tion, clean up your buckets, and pull out your taps. We made the mistake in our first year of syrup making to assume we could keep on tapping until

> **BILL'S TIP ON TAP**
> **When is the best time of year to make syrup?**
>
> *You can collect sap in the fall, as well as the early spring (but only until trees start to open their buds), but both of those timings will give you less-than-perfect sap. The sweetest sap runs at the beginning of sugar season, which is late winter.*

the sap stopped flowing. I've since learned that the later you get into syrup-making season, the more bitter and less sweet your syrup will be. The fact is, if you collect and process sap too late into the spring, you very well may wind up wasting precious money and time on syrup that no one wants to eat.

Mark Frasier, who describes himself as "a hobby sugarmaker," lives in Vermont. Mark knows a thing or two about trying to make syrup too late in the spring. When he tried to do so he noticed that the sap "smelled like dirty socks as it was boiling." No one wants to throw away precious sap, so he went ahead and processed the syrup. The result? It was so bad that he wound up throwing away every drop of the "budding syrup," as he called it. Needless to say, Mark now pulls his taps at the first signs of spring buds, and he has no plans to make "dirty sock syrup" again.

Is it time to pull your taps?

These three questions will help you know when to say goodbye to syrup season for one more year.

1. What's the weather like?

One reason you don't want to keep tapping late into the spring is the sheer lack of volume. Sap runs best when temperatures drop below freezing at night and rise into the 40s during the day. The dramatic temperatures fluctuations cause sap to freeze then thaw, building up pressure in the trees and producing productive sap runs. Sap flows at a much slower pace when temperatures warm up. Once the thermometer reads 50 at any point in the day, and/or the nights no longer reach a freezing point, you'll find you're gathering a lot less sap in your buckets.

STEPSTOOLS TO HOLSTEINS

Kayla's birth was beauty rising out of sadness. The previous fall I learned that a mother can never find a sufficient way to say goodbye to a child she's never met, but a few months after my third pregnancy was cut short, I was pregnant with Kayla. Ever since, Kayla has brought my life renewal and hope.

When she was thirteen years old, our family moved from two-tenths of an acre in suburbia to fourteen acres with an ancient farmhouse and wooded, rocky fields. Kayla and I immediately cleared land to garden. She learned to use our old cooking fireplace as it was intended and, with Bill, she repaired outbuildings for our farm animals.

Kayla started dreaming of homesteading as a toddler, armed with a stepstool and a kitchen knife. By age 15, she was growing her own vegetables, making sourdough biscuits from scratch, and caring for chickens, rabbits, ducks, and Holsteins.

Kayla's favorite thing to do with maple?

"I love to bake with maple," she says. "The Maple Blueberry Pie on page 122 is my absolute favorite of any dessert I've ever created."

2. Are your buckets empty?

By all means, do not let empty buckets be your gauge for when to pull your taps. Just because your buckets sit empty for many days in a row, do not assume the season is over. If the trees show no signs of spring buds and the forecast calls for more sap-flowing conditions, by all means, leave those taps in.

3. Does it look like spring?

Regardless of the weather forecast, it's time to stop collecting sap when you see spring buds. Unless you like the idea of wasting precious money and time on bitter syrup that destroys perfectly good blueberry pancakes, when you see spring buds you need to pack your syrup-making supplies away for another year. I know. It's hard to let go. It's hard to admit there will be no more sweet smelling golden liquid boiling in your kitchen until next winter, but embrace spring, knowing the next three seasons will include plenty of sweet maple joy thanks to all your hard work during the dark, cold days that ushered out winter. Revel in the fact that your occupation with bottling this all-natural deliciousness made those last days of winter much sweeter.

Now what?

Once the season is over, I lament that we won't be bouncing around grabbing bottles and filters in the kitchen, to the smell of maple and the sound of bubbling syrup mixed with country music, for another ten and a half months. I also feel oh-so relieved that there isn't one more heavy bucket to carry uphill, for another ten and a half months. While the cleanup is the most dreaded aspect of all of sugarmaking, I do enjoy the fact that snow has melted in some areas and I remember indeed the ground is not a permanent shade of white while we go around and pry our taps from the trees with a small claw hammer.

I remind Bill how thankful we are that we have so many trees to tap as he stands over the kitchen sink forever rinsing our numerous collection buckets with warm water—we simply use very hot water and make sure they're thoroughly air dried before stacking. I remind myself that soon enough I will again see the porch table under the continual castle of upside-down, air-drying buckets. Then I whip up some maple chocolate chip cookies because everybody needs one when feeling oh-so-sad and oh-so-relieved at the same time, am I right?

For cleaning buckets, I know some folks like to use a tiny bit of bleach. If you do so, stick with a 1:20 ratio of bleach to water and follow your cleaning with a triple rinse of hot water to make sure you've removed any trace of the cleaner. Avoid the temptation to use any other household cleaners on any of your syrup-making gear. Don't even consider cleaning your filters with anything other than very hot water. You will not be pleased with next year's syrup taste or smell if it's contaminated with cleaners.

How to clean pots at the end of the season?

Fill your dirty pots with water and a little powdered dishwasher detergent, heat to almost boiling and then let it sit overnight. After you've drained and rinsed it, fill a pot with water only and bring to a boil for 15 minutes to get rid of all cleaner residue. Never use a steel brush, steel wool, or any product containing chlorine or muriatic acid. If syrup has burnt on your pot (not that I've ever had that happen . . . ahem), use commercial cold oven cleaner. It dissolves the mess without abrasiveness. Whatever you do, be sure to thoroughly rinse your pans of all cleaning residue before you store them away as this could seriously damage the pot, maybe even making holes in it.

By the way, I didn't mention cleaning out our tubing that we've run from tree to tree because we actually don't clean those. We do bring in the shorter pieces, the ones that just connect a few trees, here and there, to buckets. Bill will stand at the kitchen sink and rinse those with hot water into a bucket then hang them over the tub to dry. For our long lines down the back hillside, we let next year's first run of sap do the cleaning for us by letting a day's worth of sap drip to the ground before we start collecting it. There are many theories in the how-to-clean-the-lines debate, but the fact is, even the Proctor Maple Research Center in Vermont doesn't have a clear-cut opinion.

Tim Perkins and Abby van den Berg of the Proctor Maple Research Center

> **MICHELLE'S TIP ON TAP**
> **My pot is all clean. Why does it still look bad?**
>
> *You probably have some "scaling" or mineral build up on your pot. Rub baking soda on it, then spray it with a mixture of ½ water, ½ vinegar. This activates the baking soda into a bubbly magical foam that should have your pot looking like new. Just rinse very well with water before you store it away for the year.*

Ryan and his wife, Lindsey Baris, now own the property his dad purchased after falling in love with its mature stand of sugar maples.

SWEET SUGGESTIONS FROM A SUGARMAKER

When Ryan Browne's dad purchased his Wisconsin property back in the 1970s, he harvested vegetable crops in the summer and maple sap in the winter. Ryan and his wife upgraded the maple operation, which today makes 150 gallons of syrup a year. Since he's a self-proclaimed "small time" sugarmaker, Ryan stores batches of syrup until he has 30–50 gallons, which he then reheats and filters into bottles all at once. An added bonus for him is that this gives his syrup opportunity for caramelization, when heated again as it's bottled.

Ryan's advice?
Start small and don't get in over your head, or you might wind up drowning in sap.

Ryan's equipment recommendation?
Ryan recommends that backyard sugarmakers ditch the coffee filters and snag a good Orlon filter. "They're washable and reusable." (Read more about filtering in chapter 3.)

Ryan's favorite recipe?
Maple fried rice. "There isn't a recipe," he says. "I never make it the same way twice. I use lots of fresh veggies—whatever I have on hand—yesterday's rice, and lots of fish sauce, in addition to maple syrup. I also try to replicate wok cooking by getting a cast iron skillet super hot and cooking small amounts of things at a time. Then I mix it all at the end."

reported this in Tubing Cleaning—Methods Used in the US (http://www.uvm.edu/~pmrc/tubing_cleaning.pdf): "A wide variety of cleaning techniques are currently used in the maple industry, including rinsing the system with pressurized air and water, or attempts to sanitize with chemical solutions such as peroxide, bleach, or alcohol. However, the effectiveness of these cleaning techniques in reducing microbial populations and increasing annual sap yield is often questionable. In fact, it is possible that many of these practices have limited, or even negative effects on sap yield." The report concludes that

HOW SUGARMAKERS USE SYRUP

"Pour maple syrup directly onto ice cream, especially vanilla. Mmm."
— Niki Miranda from Edgewood, Iowa

"Pumpkin Maple Syrup Pie is incredible! Simply replace the sugar in the recipe with syrup." —Corey Kanable from Richland Center, Wisconsin

"When I wind up with crystals in the bottom of my jar of syrup, I love using them to sweeten my tea." —Erin N. Wiseman-Parkin from Jenison, Michigan

"Maple syrup replaces sugar in my coffee."
—Matt Driessen from Kaukauna, Wisconsin

"I use maple syrup in my homemade canned applesauce instead of water and brown sugar." —Tricia Mielke Aspen from Colfax, Wisconsin

"I make an Old Fashioned with maple syrup in place of the simple syrup."
—Taylor Polak from northern Wisconsin

"I make a maple glazed rib sauce by replacing the brown sugar with maple syrup."
—Zack Cavalier from Scottdale, Pennsylvania

"I take thick-sliced bacon, marinate it overnight in pickled jalapeño juice, lay it on a cookie sheet and bake in the oven. When it's halfway done, I flip it over and brush it with maple syrup. It gets gooey and caramelized." —Vince Dean from Ashtabula, Ohio

"I love a maple Manhattan." — Jason Mangini from Morris, Connecticut

"nearly three quarters of US maple producers utilize tubing cleaning methods that are ineffective in terms of maintaining high sap yields."

Oh, and yes, our lines stay installed on our trees from one year to the next. This is a fact I didn't know when we first installed them. After that first season, I still remember Bill's look when I asked when we were going to take all the lines down. You know the look. It's the same one, with wrinkled brow and scrunched up nose, that I give a crazy person who asks if I prefer "sweet or salty."

"Call me crazy, but I really like maple syrup on buttered Brussels sprouts. Or carrots. Or turnips." —Darleen Knapp-Carvell from Parry Sound, Ontario

"It may sound weird, but I put it on cottage cheese. It's so yummy." —Micheal Kellogg from Freeport, Michigan

"Maple scallops are amazing. Bake 1 pound of scallops, 2 tablespoons of butter, and 3 tablespoons of syrup at 400° for 15 minutes, covered. Crush crackers over top and drizzle on 5 more tablespoons of syrup. Cook uncovered another 5 minutes, or until firm." —Brian Lurvey from Lancaster, New Hampshire

"I love baked sweet potatoes that are smothered in butter and then sprinkled with maple sugar. Deeeelish!" —Dameian Edgerly from Delaware, Ohio

"I put my syrup in my smoker for 3 hours, using a mix of maple and apple wood, then I use the smoked syrup on salmon; as a dipping sauce for kielbasa and other sausages; and as the main ingredient in my homemade BBQ sauce." —Josh Goldman from Stockton, New Jersey

"Over morning cereal, every single morning. From numerous cold options to warm oatmeal, it's yummy on everything." — Lucy St. Pierre from Peru, New York

"I mix it into my morning yogurt." — Kristy Hickey from Alpharetta, Georgia

"When I'm making homemade granola, I replace the honey with maple syrup. I love the richer taste." —Gretchen Kanable from Richland Center, Wisconsin

Maple syrup makes a great alternative for honey in homemade salad dressings. Whip up a whole new taste for a classic dressing in your fridge!

A Sugarmaker's Spring Cleaning Checklist

- Use a small claw hammer to pry taps from the trees. The holes will heal themselves.

- Rinse short tubing with warm water and reuse them next year.

- Flush lines if you have a pump, air compressor, or hose that you can get to your lines. Or you can leave them alone and let next year's first run of sap do the cleaning for you by letting a day's worth of sap drip to the ground before you start collecting.

- Clean all equipment thoroughly (buckets, filters, holding tanks, etc.) with hot water. Never use detergents, because they may leave a residue that will alter the taste of your syrup next year.

- Dry everything thoroughly before storing it.

MICHELLE'S TIP ON TAP
Does it matter what we call syrup?

Depending on who you're talking to, different colors and grades of syrup might be known by different names. Until recently, the same jar of syrup that was called "fancy grade" if it was bottled in Vermont, was known as "Grade A Light Amber" in the rest of the US and "No. 1, Extra Light" in Canada. Thankfully, the maple industry decided to call all maple syrup "Grade A" (because of course!) and give a few descriptive words to each color and taste that can be used to describe syrup everywhere, no matter where it's being sold. If you want go all uptown and label your syrup, you can order a grading kit, but in the end it's all syrup, which is all made with one ingredient: sap. So around here we just label it "delicious."

Now, plan on what you'll do with all that syrup.

Once spring is in full force, our buckets are all cleaned, dried, and stored away, and the pantry shelves are lined with gallons of wonderful maple syrup, it's time to start using that bad boy deliciousness. This time of year I adore any recipe that combines maple with the promise of summer. Think blueberries, lilacs, and maple. I use maple syrup in dips and dressings, as well as a friend's yummy Maple BBQ Sauce (see page 127).

When I asked some fellow sugarmakers about their favorite ways to use maple syrup all year long, I got some really great suggestions. If the list I included on pages 118–19 doesn't make you a maple addict, well you better check your pulse, friend!

MAPLE BLUEBERRY PIE

I'm not sure I should confess this, but (here I lower my head, scrunch my shoulders, and whisper ever so diminutively) I wasn't a fan of pie. Until, that is, this one entered my life. This one? I am pretty sure I could eat the whole thing. By myself. Before it's cooled from the oven. Trust me, this pie represents one of Kayla's proudest kitchen accomplishments (as she explains on page 113). She took a recipe my Daddy's cousin used to make, hidden away in an old collection of Kasecamp family recipes (thank you, Esther Galliher), tweaked it a little, and updated it with maple syrup. The result turned me into a pie-loving enthusiast and made me wish I could spend some time in Esther's kitchen.

4 cups fresh or frozen blueberries, divided
1 cup maple syrup, divided
5 tablespoons flour
⅓ cup water (or ⅓ cup blueberry juice)
1 baked pie crust

1. Preheat oven to 350°F.

2. Thaw blueberries if you're using frozen ones. I find the best way to defrost the berries is to place them in a strainer and let them drain into a bowl.

3. Mix together ⅔ cup of the maple syrup with 5 tablespoons of flour to make a paste. Set that aside while you cook 1 cup of the blueberries with ⅓ cup of syrup and ⅓ cup of water (or ⅓ cup of berry juices, if you're using frozen berries). Cook, stirring continually, on medium high until the mixture begins to thicken.

4. Then add your flour paste and the remaining blueberries. Continue stirring until thick. Pour into pie crust and bake for 11–15 minutes or longer if your filling isn't quite thick enough.

YIELDS ONE QUICKLY DISAPPEARING PIE

LILAC MAPLE SUGAR COOKIES

I'm going tell you right up front not to fret over the complex variety of sugars in this recipe. These cookies will be delicious if all you have on hand is white and brown sugar and a little maple syrup, but if you feel like whipping up a cookie with major sugar diversity and a little "wow," these cookies are for you!

½ cup butter at room temperature	1 teaspoon vanilla
¼ cup maple sugar	¼ cup oil
¼ cup white sugar	2½ cups flour
¼ cup brown sugar	1 teaspoon baking soda
1 egg yolk	1 teaspoon cream of tartar
¼ cup maple syrup	½–¾ cup lilac sugar

1. Preheat oven at 325°F.
2. Cream butter in mixer, then add in the first three types of sugars (or an equivalent amount of whatever sugars you have on hand).
3. Add the egg yolk, and cream well again. Mix in maple syrup, vanilla, and oil.
4. Sift together flour, baking soda, and cream of tartar and add to mixer slowly, until well incorporated.
5. Form dough into 1-inch balls and roll each generously in lilac sugar before placing on an ungreased cookie tray far enough apart that they won't touch after you press them out. (Feel free to substitute refined white sugar if you don't have lilac sugar, or go to SoulyRested.com for directions on making your own.) Flatten each cookie with a cookie press that you've coated in sugar.
6. Bake for 10 minutes or just until edges turn a very light brown.

YIELDS OVER 2 DOZEN COOKIES

JILL'S MAPLE BBQ SAUCE

There are so many amazing ways to incorporate maple into dressings and sauces. We must have half a dozen jars of maple-laced condiments in our fridge right now. One of them is an amazing maple BBQ sauce that my friend, Jill Winger, out on the Wyoming prairie introduced me to. If you haven't met Jill, check out her heritage cooking recipes on ThePrairieHomestead.com. Oh, and take liberties with this recipe. More vinegar, less molasses—whatever makes it perfect for your family's tastebuds.

2 cups tomato sauce
   (or one 14.5 oz can)
1 can (6 oz) of tomato paste
⅓ cup apple cider vinegar
¼ cup real maple syrup
¼ cup molasses
2 tablespoons Worcestershire sauce
1 teaspoon garlic powder
1 teaspoon paprika
1 teaspoon Dijon mustard

½ teaspoon onion powder
½ teaspoon salt
½ teaspoon black pepper
1–2 teaspoons liquid smoke
   (optional, but nice if you're wanting
   the smoky flavor)
⅛ teaspoon cayenne pepper
   (optional—use only if you want a
   kick)

1. Combine all ingredients in a medium saucepan, and bring to a simmer over medium heat. Stir and simmer for 10–15 minutes, so all the tastes can meld together.

2. Transfer your BBQ sauce to a jar and store it in the refrigerator for several weeks. You can also freeze it if you'd like to keep it longer.

3. To use your sauce, mix into ground beef before you shape it into patties. Or pour it over chicken breasts, legs, or thighs before grilling. Use it as a glaze or mix-in for meatloaf. Enjoy it as a sauce on homemade BBQ pizza. Or serve it on Maple Pulled Pork Sandwiches (page 162).

YIELDS 3 CUPS

Try Something Different

TAP INTO SUGAR MAPLE ALTERNATIVES
IN EVERY SINGLE STATE

Despite the rocky fields and almost unusable terrain of our little homestead, it does have an old coop that offers shelter for our chickens in the rough New England winter winds, a barn that's always active with the antics of our farm animals, and sugar maples that offer us sweet sap as every winter reaches an end. Even so, if we didn't have one sugar maple, we would still have alternatives to tap. In this chapter, I'll help you determine if you might as well.

When North America was first colonized, sugar maples were, by far, the most prevalent broadleaf trees in the areas that went on to become the syrup-producing regions. Thus, by nature of being the first source for syrup, sugar maples have become synonymous with syrup. While there is no denying that they were the first, or that they do produce the most sugar-laden sap, sugar maples are far from the only trees that make delicious all-natural sweeteners. You may be surprised that even if you don't own a sugar maple you may have many trees that are good for tapping right in your own backyard.

If so, you'll find that those other varieties of trees also produce syrup with different hints of flavor—some more "earthy," some even slightly resembling butterscotch—yum! In fact, some trees even offer advantages over sugar maples, such as walnut trees, which can be tapped at a much younger age than sugar maples. I've compiled this list after talking with numerous sugarmakers across the country and even around the world. Overall, I've come to the conclusion that nothing beats a sugar maple, so if you have plenty of those you may not want to bother with anything else. Mark and Kim

Sap can be collected successfully from numerous varieties of trees in the maple, birch, and walnut families.

Oldenburgh, for example, are backyard sugarmakers in Maine, where they have about 100 maple trees to tap, so they allow their neighbors to plunder their birch sap, in exchange for a few birch syrup whoopie pies. Kim reports that she prefers maple over the dark flavored syrup her neighbors make, but the birch whoopie pies are delicious! (See page 144 for a yummy recipe using birch syrup.)

So rest assured, you do not need to have sugar maples or live in New England to make amazing syrup. Live in the mid-Atlantic area? Maybe you have a sycamore you could tap. Live on the West Coast? Look for some bigleaf maples. Virginia? Search for black walnut. Since sap can be collected quite successfully from numerous varieties of trees in the maple, birch, and walnut families, and since among these three tappable species at least one can be found in every state except Hawaii, you may have some very sweet reasons to read this chapter thoroughly, no matter where you live. Oh, and if you do happen to live in the 50th state, wait until you see what tropical tree made it into this chapter because folks have figured out how to lance its flower to make syrup!

What trees can be tapped for syrup?

Here's a list of many trees, which grow in various climates and can be tapped for syrup. While I'm sure this list is not exhaustive, I hope it inspires you to tap into the resources you may have right in your own backyard.

Maple varieties

Maples, overall, are great trees to tap. Specifically, sugar maples produce the largest quantity of sap and the sweetest quality of syrup of all deciduous trees.

In truth, any species of maple will make a great syrup. Not many maples can be found in warmer climates, but that is mainly due to lack of moisture, not height of temperature. In fact, maples can tolerate a high level of heat, just not if it is compounded with persistent drought. Boxelders and canyon maples are a few varieties that have managed to survive where other maples do not.

Sugar maple (*Acer saccharum*)

This is the holy grail of maples because it's a rather common tree and its sap is more concentrated than any other maple, meaning you can make more syrup with less sap. Can I get an "Amen"?

WHAT'S SO SPECIAL ABOUT A SUGAR MAPLE?

Aside from the fact that they produce the most sap with the highest sugar content of any tree, here are lots of interesting tidbits about sugar maples that make them pretty special:

- Their vibrant fall color ranges from bright yellow to orange to fluorescent red-orange. In fact, one sugar maple tree may display all the colors at one time!

- A sugar maple can live for more than 400 years! (But you have to wait 40 years after planting before you'll have a tree big enough to tap. In fact, sugar maples won't even flower for at least two decades after they're planted.)

- The slow-growing, long-lived sugar maple grows to be 75 feet tall in culti-vated areas, but it has been found as tall as 120 feet in the wild!

- The hard wood of a sugar maple tree is close-grained and sought after for furniture making, especially "bird's-eye maple." This type of grain (which is so named because its tiny circles resemble birds' eyes) can be found in various hard woods, but is by far most common in sugar maples.

- Native Americans stored maple sugar in bark boxes and made a sweet sauce with it for many of their foods.

- The sugar maple is the state tree for more states than any other species. New York, West Virginia, Wisconsin, and Vermont all claim it.

- The Latin name for sugar maple (*Acer saccharum*) reflects its strength as well as its sweetness. *Acer* (Latin for "sharp") refers to the fact that Romans fashioned their spear handles with strong maple wood. *Saccharum* (Latin for "sugar") is self-explanatory.

Black maple (*Acer nigrum*)

These trees rival sugar maples in sap volume, and they resemble them as well. Like a sugar maple, black maple leaves have a smooth margin, but black maple leaves tend to have only 3 lobes, versus the common 5 lobes of a sugar maple. They also have much shallower, wider areas between the lobes of their leaves, not creating the "u" shape of sugar maple leaves but a stretched out shallow valley

from one lobe to the next. Other ways to distinguish black maples? Compared to sugar maples, black maples have larger clumps of spring buds, darker bark color, drooping leaves, and hairier lower leaf surfaces. From what I'm told, black maples can tolerate extreme weather better than sugar maples, both drought and short-term flooding, but since a black maple's sap is nearly as sweet and abundant as a sugar maple's, in the end, who cares which it is. Just tap it and make some wonderful syrup!

Red maple (*Acer rubrum*)

While they also produce high yields of sap, these maples are the first to bud in the spring. They're well-named, given that every identifiable part of red maples are crimson. From the buds to the spring blooms, from the twigs to the leaf stems and then the fall foliage, the red hue makes identification pretty easy. The hard part with red maples is the fact that you'll have to pull your taps early in

spring. Since sap tastes bitter once trees start to bud, the syrup season of a red maple is shorter than others. Dameian Edgerly, who taps the four red maples in his backyard in central Ohio, says the short season is worth it for the delicious, slightly tart flavor of red maple syrup. His four trees yield around a gallon of syrup a year.

Silver maple (*Acer saccharinum*)

Since these trees, similar to the red maple, produce spring buds very early, their tapping season is shorter than many other trees, but they make a fine syrup. To identify a silver maple leaf, look for a pale, silver underside and deep notches between the lobes. Corey Kanable, of Wisconsin, uses a mixture of sugar and silver maple sap every year and feels that the addition of silver maple

sap makes for a sweeter tasting syrup and a stronger maple flavor. Scott Cherek, on the other hand, has only silver maples in his yard in southeastern Wisconsin, and he feels that silver maples make for a slightly lighter flavored syrup. "With my 3 silver maples, I collect as much as 150 gallons of sap and make 4 gallons of syrup every year."

Norway maple (*Acer platanoides*)

While most people agree that Norway maples don't make syrup as sweet as sugar maples, they seem to be a pretty good alternative. Roland Jordan taps 30 Norway maples every year in Rhode Island. He enjoys his Norway syrup and describes it as having "a nice buttery flavor." To know if your maple is a sugar or a Norway, just look at how pointy each and every tip of the leaf is. On a sugar maple, only the apexes of the 5 lobes are sharp,

while other tips are blunt. A Norway maple leaf is sharp at every tip. Other distinguishing characteristics include a horizontal samara (think coat-hanger shape as opposed to the horse-shoe shape of a sugar maple samara) and milky fluid that is released when a leaf is removed from a stem.

Gorosoe maple (*Acer mono*)

The gorosoe (commonly known as a painted maple) is a maple tree that grows throughout eastern Asia. While it is native to Japan, Korea, China, Mongolia, and the Russian Far East, it's most popular in Korea. In fact, "gorosoe" is the Korean word for "good for the bones," and that's a perfect name by Korean standards. A *New York Times* article called "The Forests of Southern Korea Yield a Prized Elixir" by Choe Sang-Hun published on February 24, 2009, explained how the Koreans prize maple in a different form than we do. Instead of going to all the hard work of boiling, filtering, and bottling maple syrup, Koreans enjoy the gorosoe sap as a refreshing, healthy drink, straight from the tree. I'm not talking a few little sips, or even a cup full. When they do some sap drinking, they do some serious sap drinking. The *Times* article explained that the gorosoe sap is part of an intense spiritual ritual for the Koreans, which has probably been around for thousands of years, that involves drinking five gallons of gorosoe sap in one sitting. To make the effort of downing so much liquid in one sitting a little more doable, the Koreans like to do so in heated rooms that encourage sweating, while eating lots of salty snacks that encourage thirst. As science uncovers new reasons to love maple sap, and as maple syrup is becoming famous for its health benefits, Korean government officials have wisely planned gorosoe festivals for tourists to introduce foreigners to this health-based ritual and improve the income of villagers in mountainous areas that are home to many gorosoe trees.

Boxelder (*Acer negundo*)

Not only does this tree confuse me because it goes by many names—from Manitoba maple to elf maple—but it's also confusing to identify. Many homeowners confuse boxelder leaves with poison ivy because of its three leaflets. To be reassured that you have a boxelder, just notice if the leaves are directly opposite each other on

the branch. If not—if the leaves alternate—then you may have stumbled upon some poison ivy. Officially, boxelder is in the maple family (kind of a cousin to the sugar maple) but with its compound leaf and crazy-growing branches, it doesn't look like a maple tree at all. Because it's a hardy tree, and it frequently grows in abandoned areas—along railroad tracks, and in ditches—this may be a sugarmaking tree you can easily find. If you do, make sure you have a great way to transport the sap home, because a boxelder requires a greater sap-to-syrup ratio than a sugar maple, and it typically produces up to 4 times as much sap. If you don't mind investing a fair amount of time and money into boiling your sap, you can make a decent amount of delicious syrup. According to Scott Hofer, a backyard sugarmaker in Manitoba, Canada, the taste of boxelder syrup is second to none, although he refers to them as Manitoba maples in his neck of the woods.

Bigleaf maple (*Acer macrophyllum*)
The bigleaf maple is a tree of many names, sometimes called a Pacific Coast maple or the Oregon maple, that grows in British Columbia, Washington, Oregon, and California. As Gary Backlund, author of *Bigleaf Sugaring*, explains, "Bigleaf maple is one of the most plentiful softwood tree species in North America, so

there's no shortage of trees for tapping." And Backlund fancies his bigleaf syrup. He describes the taste as "stronger than eastern maple syrup, with a caramel undertone."

Pamela Williams has been tapping bigleafs on Vancouver Island, off the west coast of Canada, for almost a decade. She explains that she varies her number of taps anywhere from 35 to 100 or more, depending on the year, because the West Coast sap flow, in general, is pretty unpredictable. Pamela will start with a few dozen taps and see how much sap is flowing from her bigleaf maples before she commits to 100 taps and winds up in over her head with sap flow, but she loves her bigleaf syrup. She says it's slightly thicker than sugar maple syrup, and the flavor is a more concentrated maple taste.

While Native Americans have tapped bigleaf maple trees for centuries, an enthusiastic group of bigleaf syrup makers, the Vancouver Island Sapsuckers, is working to make the idea popular once again. The Sapsuckers help newbies on the island find their sugarmaking legs, so to speak, but word is finally spreading off-island as well, with a growing number of north Pacific Coast sugarmakers surfacing every year. In fact, Gary Bucklund estimates there are well over 10,000 people producing bigleaf maple syrup in British Columbia. If you are one of those newbies who is considering tapping some bigleaf maples, be prepared early. Syrup season can start in November and it will run, off and on, until March, but don't expect 4 months' worth of sap. Instead, you'll find you have 2–5 mini seasons in that 4-month window. You'll find that the trees need to be retapped every 3–6 weeks as well. (See page 53 for more information on re-tapping.) Plus, if you're tapping bigleafs, you'll occasionally be swimming in sap. On the best days of a season, Pamela has gathered as much as 6 gallons of sap from a single tap. While it's rare, a large flow like that can happen for up to a full week at a time, but bigleaf sugarmakers don't have to sacrifice quality for quantity. Pamela says the average bigleaf sugar content runs from 1½ percent to 2 percent, rivaling a sugar maple.

Canyon maple, or bigtooth maple (*Acer grandidentatum*)

The canyon maple is primarily found throughout canyons in the Rocky Mountain states. Maples require a good amount of moisture, which can be in short supply in the West in the summer months, except for the wetter areas in the canyons and ravines. While the canyon maple sap has a high sugar content, the volume isn't so great. For that reason, I'm guessing there may never be commercially produced canyon maple syrup, but if you have one in your backyard, your family sure could enjoy collecting some sap. (Although if Dulce East has made a successful business out of Alaskan birch syrup, who knows what someone may do with canyon maple syrup someday. Read Dulce's story on page 144.)

This same species is also found in Texas, where it is known by a different common name. In the Lone Star state, folks know it as bigtooth maple. Dr. Mark Vorderbruggen, a research chemist in Texas, has recorded tapping maples in Houston and getting decent amounts of sap without a typical freeze-thaw cycle, which would be hard to come by in Texas.

Rocky Mountain maple (*Acer glabrum*)

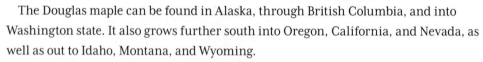

The Plateau Native Americans made syrup from these trees, mostly found in western North America. They don't look like typical maple trees, but more like large shrubs. If you live in the West, this may be the most likely maple candidate for you to find to tap, so I'm going to list all varieties that can be used for syrup making:

The Rocky Mountain maple grows in eastern California, Nevada, and Utah.

The Douglas maple can be found in Alaska, through British Columbia, and into Washington state. It also grows further south into Oregon, California, and Nevada, as well as out to Idaho, Montana, and Wyoming.

Greene's maple can be found in central California.

The New Mexico maple grows in its namesake state as well as Arizona, Colorado, and Utah.

Sycamore maple (*Acer pseudoplatanus*)

While most Europeans think they don't have the ability to tap trees for syrup, this species of maple tree, which is native to central and southern Europe (but can be found in pockets of the US and Canada as well), proves that theory wrong. Kevin Koppensteiner, who taps his sycamore maples in Austria, says that while the sycamore maple sap has a pretty low sugar content (about 1 percent), the work is definitely worth it. Kevin's wife agrees. At first

she wasn't too crazy about the money
her husband was spending to set up a
field kitchen to make maple syrup in
an area where no one thought he could.
Once she tasted the delicious results,
however, she was fully on board with
Kevin's new hobby. Both Kevin and
his wife agree, sycamore maple syrup
is delicious, with hints of caramel and
vanilla.

BILL'S TIP ON TAP
Am I destroying the value of my trees and potential lumber if I tap them?

In many ways, yes, that is possible, depending on the trees you're considering tapping, but tap hole maple lumber is becoming an interesting, desired lumber in its own right, so I personally enjoy my syrup with no guilt at all about declining lumber values.

Walnut varieties

While their sugar content rivals maples, most walnut trees produce much less sap.
Another problem with tapping walnuts—especially black walnuts—is that their wood can
be very valuable as timber, but scars from tapping may devalue the lumber. Because walnut trees are notoriously messy—from heavy pollen and annoying catkins in the spring
to messy nuts and the troublesome squirrels those nuts attract all summer and fall—and
they can be toxic to nearby gardens, many people aren't walnut fans. However these
trees can be found in significant numbers in the mid-Atlantic and midwestern states,
where there aren't as many maples, and they offer a sweet, nutty tasting syrup.

Butternut/white walnut (*Juglans cinerea*)

Known for its edible nuts and gorgeous lumber,
the butternut aligns closely with the sugar maple
for sugar content and volume of sap. Butternut
syrup has a nutty taste, with a hint of fruitiness.
If you're lucky enough to have one of these trees
to tap, just beware of the high pectin levels in
the sap. Be sure to filter the pectin out, unless
you want butternut jelly when you're done boiling. Be sure to plant a few new trees with your
butternut seeds, because this gem of a tree is
becoming quite rare.

Black walnut (*Juglans nigra*)

The black walnut offers a long tapping season that Jane McNaughton takes advantage of in Pennsylvania. Jane insists that the mess, and the lower amount of sap, doesn't faze her, because the syrup is that good. Craig Waters has been tapping black walnut trees for a few years in Wisconsin. He describes the taste as distinctly like butterscotch, but does warn that filtering the pectin can be a bear.

Mat Cabral, a presenter at the first-ever Southern Syrup Symposium in West Virginia, in 2018, makes black walnut syrup. He recommends you save your sap for a few weeks—making sure to keep it cold, around 32–34°F. In that time, most of the pectin will separate from the sap, enabling you to scoop it out easily.

Heartnut (*Juglans ailantifolia*)

While heartnuts have a good concentration of sugar in their sap, they produce much less sap than maples.

English walnut (*Juglans regia*)

These trees produce the walnuts we purchase from the grocery store, and some folks make delicious syrup from them as well.

The biggest challenge to walnut syrup is filtering the pectin. If you're able to keep your sap cool for many days, the majority of the pectin will separate and can be scooped out before boiling.

Birch varieties

Birch sap spoils rapidly, so you'll have to process it quickly. And you'll need at least 100, if not 110, gallons of sap to make 1 gallon of syrup. The slightly warmer weather that ends the maple syrup season actually signals the beginning of the birch season, so a sugarmaker can tap both maple and birch, one after the other. Another big difference with birch trees is their size. While experts recommend not tapping other varieties of trees that are smaller than 10 inches in diameter, birch trees are naturally small and short lived, so birch trees as small as 5 inches in diameter are often tapped. Worldwide, not much birch syrup is being made, but birch sap is prized in Russia and areas of northern Europe as a nutritious drinking water that offers more minerals and antioxidants than sugar maples' sap. So if you can collect some and keep it cold simply for drinking, it's a worthy endeavor even if you never want to take on the challenge of making birch syrup.

> ### BILL'S TIP ON TAP
> **How much sap do I need to collect to make a good amount of syrup?**
>
> *It depends on what kind of tree you're tapping, as well as other factors, but in general a sugar maple will produce 1 gallon of syrup for every 40 gallons of sap that you collect, filter, boil, and bottle. On a really good day, from a really good sugar maple, we can collect 5–10 gallons of sap. That means one sugar maple tree, in one day, in the absolute ideal situations, will give you enough sap to make 2–4 cups of syrup.*

Paper birch (*Betula papyrifera*)

The paper birch offers the sweetest sap of all birch varieties. Paul Giencke, a stonemason by profession, taps paper birch in northwestern Wisconsin. He compares the taste of his syrup to sarsaparilla or root beer and testifies that it makes excellent glaze on salmon or pork, but he can also testify, from personal experience, that any sap not boiled the day it's collected will smell nasty the next day. "It's putrid," he says.

Yellow birch (*Betula alleghaniensis*)

The yellow birch sugar content can be as low as .5 percent (yes, ½ of 1 percent), meaning you would need to filter and boil down 180 gallons of yellow birch sap to make one gallon of yellow birch syrup, but Jim Jessup is glad to go to the effort in his backyard in western New York state. Jim makes all his syrup from yellow birch, and he and his wife

love the "really rich flavor that's very different than maple, but good in its own way."

Black birch (*Betula lenta*)

This variety, native to eastern North America, is most commonly used to make birch beer. Mark Frasier, who operates a sawmill in Vermont by day and boils syrup in his backyard by night, made birch syrup one year by tapping all his black birch, along with his white and yellow birch trees too. He mixed the three varieties of birch sap and made syrup that tasted similar to molasses.

River birch (*Betula nigra*)

This birch tree grows in the southeastern and northeastern areas of the United States. This variety has bark that peels off in sheets, similar to a paper birch tree. A huge fact in favor of this variety of birch is that it's resistant to the bronze birch borer.

Gray birch (*Betula populifolia*)

Brett McLeod, author of *The Woodland Homestead*, was despondent when he realized not one sugar maple graced his property. But he knew there were other opportunities for food from his forest—gray birch to be exact—and Brett describes his alternative syrup as "wonderful."

European white birch (*Betula pendula*)

While this tree is grown as an ornamental in the United States, European white birch can be tapped for syrup. I've talked to only one gentleman who actually made white birch syrup, and he explained that he would never do it again. He personally found the taste unappealing, to put it nicely. Yet I talked to him long before I talked with my new Alaskan friend and birch

syrup maker, Dulce East (see page 144), who helped me understand the many ways it's easy for well-meaning, knowledgeable sugarmakers to mess up birch syrup, so I didn't know to ask him a few important details about his process. Still, even poorly processed birch syrup has a redeeming quality: You can use it for marinating meat, cooking and baking, and as a substitute for vanilla in baking. Can I get an "mmm"?

Alaskan white birch (*Betula neoalaskana*)

If you decide to tap Alaskan white birch, don't be convinced that you should finish at a lower Brix to avoid bitterness. Anything less than 66 percent sugar and your product is not syrup. I have talked to folks who bottle their birch syrup at 60 percent Brix, but they don't have birch syrup, they just have birch-flavored water.

Dulce and Michael East's world-renowned birch syrup company started when two newlyweds tapped a few birch trees.

SWEET SUGGESTIONS FROM A SUGARMAKER

The Easts tap about 16,000 Alaskan white birch trees every year. Dulce explains that each tree results in only about 12 ounces of birch syrup per year. She describes her birch syrup as "rich, complex, and spicy-sweet, reminiscent of sorghum, honey, or molasses, with hints of berries, citrus, chocolate, and coffee."

Dulce's advice?

"Expect to work hard. While it's rewarding, there's no denying that making syrup from sap is challenging (with any tree, but even more so with birch)."

Dulce's tool recommendation?

A digital refractometer, because measuring the Brix is so important and because "hydrometers are a bit old-school and can be difficult to use." (See pages 91–93 for a detailed explanation of both tools.)

Dulce's favorite recipe?

Baked Birch-Nut Squash

1. Cut 2 Delicata squash in half and scoop out seeds. Bake 30 minutes at 350°F.

2. Melt 2 tablespoons of butter in pan, add 1 diced apple, 2 tablespoons birch syrup or birched honey, ¼ teaspoon cinnamon, ¼ teaspoon ginger, and ⅓ cup chopped pecans and simmer for 5 minutes.

3. Spoon mixture into squash and bake 20 minutes or until tender.

Sycamore and sweetgum varieties

The sycamore and the sweetgum trees are both in the same family and are really easy to identify. The sycamore has maple-like leaves and a trunk that looks a little like green, tan, and cream camouflage. The sweetgum has beautiful, unique, star-shaped leaves and brown, spikey fruit balls.

Sycamore (*Platanus occidentalis*)

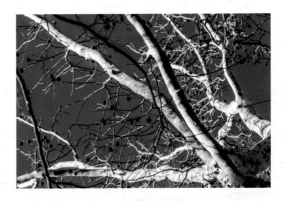

Not to be confused with the sycamore maple (on page 138), this tree also has a much lower sugar content than a sugar maple, and it produces a syrup that some describe as having a touch of butterscotch, honey, or caramel flavor. Any of those options works for me. Yet others I've talked to say sycamore is the "syrup of last resort," explaining that it's not a taste they like. Regardless of where one falls on the love-hate spectrum, not many would argue that sycamore sap can definitely be blended with others, adding a butterscotch undertone to the final syrup. As an added bonus, if you own a sycamore tree, you own a long-lived, hardy tree. Many sycamores live for five to six hundred years.

Of course, in reality, most people have never heard of tapping sycamore, so there is a wealth of delicious sycamore sap around the country just waiting to be tapped into. Because of its lower sugar content, as well as its uniqueness, sycamore sap can bring in a pretty penny for a sugarmaker who is eager to give sycamore syrup a try.

Paul Hovan, a sugarmaker in Vermont, explains that you're lucky to have 1 percent sugar content with sycamore, so it takes at least 100 gallons of sap to make a gallon of syrup and a vacuum system is a must, in his opinion. He describes his sycamore syrup as having a "molasses" flavor, but explains that when he boils his sap down a little farther, there's a butterscotch undertone.

Sweetgum (*Liquidambar styraciflua*)
While there's very little published about the sweetgum's sugar content or syrup quality, it's a beautiful tree that grows well in southern regions. I've heard it offers quality syrup, but it does not offer a lot of sap wood in relation to heart wood. It also has a thick resin, which must make filtering challenging.

Other varieties (no tapping required)

Palm (*Caryota urens*)
It turns out palm trees are not really trees at all, but flowering plants. If you happen to live in the only one of all 50 US states that doesn't have a truly tappable tree (and that's Hawaii), believe it or not, you can still make syrup. Palm syrup is not made by boiling sap, but by lancing the flower of the palm, to make it weep. The liquid collected from the flower is boiled down to a syrup that, I'm told, is wonderfully sweet, the hue and consistency of honey. Since palm flowers are only in bloom a few weeks of every year, palm syrup production offers one of the shortest windows you'll find. Even so, retiring sugarmakers may want to migrate toward this warm-weather syrup alternative and set up a little tiki hut under palm tree flowers, no?

Shagbark hickory (*Carya ovata*)

Hickory syrup isn't typically made by tapping into the trunk of the tree. Instead, hickory syrup is made from an extract taken from the bark of these trees. Yep, you literally toast bark pieces in the oven, then boil them to get an extract. After adding some sugar, you simmer your sugared extract until it's the consistency you want, and voila, you have hickory syrup without ever firing up a big pot of sap or doing one ounce of filtering, which pleases fans of hickory syrup. Mike Farrell, former director of Cornell's Uihlein Maple Forest research center, also suggests boiling down your bark pieces in maple, birch, or walnut sap or adding maple sugar instead of refined when you simmer your extract if you want to make a gourmet, marketable item out of shagbark hickory syrup.

Tulip poplar (*Liriodendron tulipifera*)

Poplar syrup is made the same way as hickory syrup, by boiling down toasted pieces of poplar bark.

Sorghum

So, yeah, sorghum isn't a tree, but sorghum syrup—a favorite in the South—is worth a mention here. The all-natural molasses-like syrup is made by pressing sorghum canes through a mill to extract the green, extra-sweet juices out of the cane when the tall stalks are ready to harvest, typically in mid-September.  I happened to be in Tennessee last sorghum season, enjoyed helping in the harvest of some sorghum, and later picked up a jar of sorghum syrup in a tiny country store. As I paid the gentlemen with an accent as sweet as his wares, he told me that the right name for sorghum syrup is "molasses." I argued that molasses is a byproduct of the sugar industry. Sorghum, on the other hand, is juice extracted directly from the sorghum cane—I'd just harvested and tasted the ambrosial juice myself earlier that day.

When I tasted that jar of sorghum syrup, I understood why he was adamant. Folks, call it what you want, sorghum syrup tastes like molasses. I'm sorry to say I sacrificed a perfectly good pancake to it. Even Bixby turned his nose up at it. The rest of my sorghum syrup was a perfect all-natural alternative to molasses in the kitchen. See the recipe on page 205 for the proof in the pudding, or should I say the proof in the popcorn?

Make this syrup without sap

Making syrup from trees in your own backyard is extremely rewarding—not to mention sweetly delicious. While I have never tried my hand at all the alternative ways of making syrup explained on the last few pages, like toasting hickory bark or lancing palm flowers, I have often made another alternative kind of syrup that truly anyone can make. Every spring I love making ambrosial purple syrup made from, believe it or not, the delicate, aromatic blooms of the lilac bush.

As sugaring season draws to a close, while there is still a foot of snow on the ground, emerging lilac buds promise warm weather will again return to our homestead. As

Kombucha is a fermented tea, with an active culture, that people have been making for thousands of years. I flavor ours with fruit and maple syrup, but one of my favorite sweeteners is lilac syrup.

Jars filled with alternating layers of sugar and lilac blooms produce a wonderful floral sugar in just a few short weeks.

warmer days usher in May, green buds are transformed into deep-purple promises. Then, day by day, a few new blooms open with each morning and glisten under spring raindrops. While there's no denying that the blooms are wonderful in their own right, lilac flowers are also inspiration for some wonderful alternative sweeteners, from lilac sugar, to lilac honey, to the most glorious, sweet, delicious lilac syrup. Yes, syrup.

Before I had any idea of the floral confections I'd one day be making with my lilacs on my 200-year-old homestead, they first offered a wonderful history lesson.

The history of the lilac bush

Lilac bushes bathe corners of our farmhouse and edges of our farm with deeply perfumed color every spring, but the ones by the front door are my favorite. I linger in their shade and wonder who else may have done the same over the past two centuries.

A photo we inherited with our house has the year "1900" scrawled across the back in faint, long strokes.

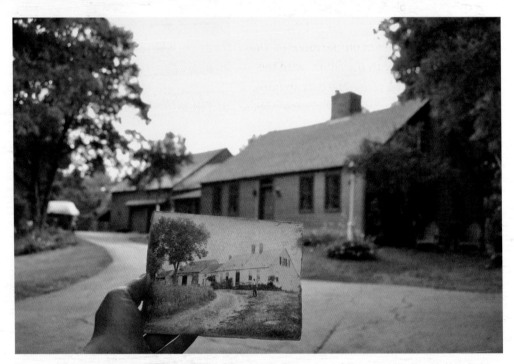

The image of our home from the late 1800s shows my favorite maple tree was beautifully mature even then. My lilac, on the front corner of our home, may have been there as well.

Indeed, these lusciously blooming branches may be from the original lilacs planted in that very spot 200 years ago, when our home was new. You see, when our home was built, it was customary to have lilacs by the front door, so guests could enjoy their scent when entering. They were a new, hardy shrub brought over from England at the time. They lost favor as time went on, and many homeowners preferred newer varieties of flowering bushes that offered longer bloom time.

When I came across this tidbit of history–that it was popular to plant fragrant lilacs by the front door–I immediately inspected the two old photographs I have of our farmhouse. One photo we inherited with the house, with the year "1900" scrawled across the back in faint, long strokes. In that picture, the photographer was more interested in showing the deep wagon wheel ruts in the dirt road and the old stone walls of the little bridge than our home, which sits off in the blurry distance, but there is definitely a tall, leggy bush at the front, right corner of our cape, in the same spot where our branches of purple joy stand today.

The other image came to us a few years ago. It's older than the first image and shows a hardworking farmer standing in the drive, coming out to greet the photographer. I feel so privileged to know the name of the farmer—Asa—because the image was delivered to our door one sunny Saturday afternoon last summer by the woman who had married Asa's great grandson. I like to stare into Asa's content gaze and imagine his parents choosing his name after the good king of Judah. I also imagine his parents teaching young Asa about his namesake, and I wonder if he too loved the verse that I love from the records of Asa, "The eyes of the Lord range throughout the earth to strengthen those whose hearts are fully committed to him."

Asa's old sap bucket has a simpler job these days, no longer collecting maple sap, but holding stories it can never tell me.

I glance at this picture pretty often. It welcomes guests to our home, printed on a slate plaque on our front porch. I can glance over my shoulder to the barn as it looks today and back to Asa's barn as it looked in the 1800s. The fact is, our barn was old when Asa posed for the photographer.

I wonder about all the hands throughout the years that may have nurtured my lilacs and tapped my maples, and I am thankful that today it is my hands that are working on this homestead.

An ambrosial experiment

Kayla has taught me to assume everything has multiple uses, and I started wondering if savory smelling lilacs could be turned into a sweet dessert. We delved into an ambrosial experiment together, years ago. The result—making syrup with lilacs—was much easier than our extravagant maple syrup production.

Of course, it is also an entirely different outcome. While I call it "syrup," for lack of a better term, it's a much thinner consistency than true syrup. It's a simple syrup. While I do enjoy the sweet, floral liquid on a plate of pancakes, I prefer it as a flavorful sweetener for warm and cold drinks, an amazing addition to the second ferment stage of my kombucha that I brew continually, or an extravagant topping on a bowl of vanilla ice cream.

Lilac syrup is a pleasant light yellow-green if I don't add a few blueberries to tint it a pretty shade of purple.

LILAC SYRUP

To make lilac syrup, on a warm, sun-kissed May day, we clip enough blooms to fill a large vase. This is always about twice as much as we need, so the rest grace a window ledge or mantle. We separate the purple blossoms from their green sepals and yellow pistils. They slide off effortlessly. In only a few minutes we have a cupful.

We boil water, add sugar and the blooms, and let it simmer for 10 minutes. I'll add five or six blueberries too, if I have some in the freezer, to make for a beautiful purple-colored syrup. If I don't have any blueberries, the syrup still tastes wonderful. It's just more of a light yellow-green hue.

1 cup water

1 cup sugar

1 cup lilac blooms

5–6 fresh or frozen blueberries (optional)

1. Heat water and sugar until sugar is dissolved. Add lilac flowers and simmer for 10 minutes. If desired, add a few blueberries for color.

2. Filter the syrup into a glass jar to remove the flowers. Let it cool, then keep refrigerated. Water bath can your lilac syrup if you'd like to keep it through the winter.

YIELDS 1¾ CUPS

NICE-N-SLOW MAPLE CHICKEN AND RICE

Slow cooker meals make the house smell amazing, save energy, and bring me such joy at dinner time when—in a matter of minutes—a hot meal is on the table. Add maple to the mix and everything is even better.

2 pounds boneless chicken breasts

1 cup maple syrup

½ cup yellow mustard

3 tablespoons brown sugar

4 tablespoons Worcestershire sauce

For additional sauce:

½ cup maple syrup

1 tablespoon mustard

1 tablespoon brown sugar

3 tablespoons Worcestershire sauce

> *Don't have time for "slow" and want to use a pressure cooker instead? Cut the raw chicken into smaller chunks and plan on it taking about 25 minutes in the pressure cooker. If it doesn't look quite done, just cook it for an additional 5 minutes on manual. (Because the meat will be nice and hot at that point, the pot will come up to pressure quickly the second time.)*

1. Place the chicken breasts in the slow cooker.

2. Whisk the remaining ingredients together, and pour over the chicken. Cook on low for 6–7 hours or high for 3–3½ hours.

3. With two forks, pull the chicken apart into fine strips of meat (it will do this almost effortlessly) then toss it back in the crock pot, coating it in the juices, and serve over rice. This also makes a yummy pulled chicken sandwich.

Option: The extra sauce is not always necessary. I just sometimes find that the meat soaks up all the juices, in which case I warm up a little extra maple sauce to pour over the rice and chicken in the serving bowls.

YIELDS 6-8 SERVINGS

MAPLE PORK STIR-FRY

When friends hear you're writing a book about maple that's going to include some recipes, a few of them are bound to reach out to you with a yummy suggestion, or 3 or 4. The minute I tasted this unique, slightly sweet stir-fry, I knew I had to include "Aunt" Ann's friend's recipe. She's from Canada, the land of maple.

1 tablespoon cooking oil

1 pound pork tenderloin, cut into thin strips

½ medium onion, sliced

1 cup snap peas

2 small apples, sliced

5 tablespoons maple syrup, divided

¾ cup balsamic vinaigrette dressing, divided

Salt and pepper, to taste

2 cups cooked brown rice

1. Heat one tablespoon of cooking oil in a large wok or skillet.

2. Add pork and onions. Once pork is cooked through, remove from skillet and keep warm.

3. Add rest of ingredients to skillet, reserving a few tablespoons of the syrup and ¼ cup of the dressing. Stir-fry until vegetables are tender, but still crisp.

4. Return meat to skillet. Add the last of the syrup and dressing, add salt and pepper, and heat through before serving over rice.

This recipe works well with chicken as well. You can substitute frozen stir-fry vegetables in place of the snap peas and apples.

YIELDS 4 SERVINGS

SLOPPY MAPLE SANDWICHES

These sandwiches are seriously as simple as a meal can get. While you may have to hold back the hungry mob while the maple-infused sauce is warming in your skillet, the good news is that once the meat is cooked, the meal is ready in minutes.

2 pounds ground meat

4 cloves minced garlic

1 cup ketchup

1 cup tomato sauce

4 tablespoons maple syrup

5 tablespoons Worcestershire sauce

1 tablespoon prepared mustard

1 teaspoon garlic powder

1 teaspoon onion powder

Pepper to taste

1. Brown and drain 2 pounds of ground meat. I like to use extra-lean turkey.
2. Add garlic and lightly sauté with meat.
3. Add the remaining ingredients and heat through. That's it.

Options: Feel free to substitute a cup of fresh or canned crushed tomatoes in place of the tomato sauce. It lends a different consistency to the meat, and you'll probably want to up the amount of seasonings just a bit if you do.

Another option is to sauté some chopped onion and green pepper before browning your meat. If you'd like to intensify the flavors, heat the sauce ingredients together in your pan and let them simmer a little before adding in your browned meat.

You can make an extra-large batch of the sauce and freeze or can it in single-meal servings for some extra-easy meals.

YIELDS ROUGHLY A DOZEN SANDWICHES

MAPLE PULLED PORK SANDWICHES

My whole family loves these sandwiches. Feel free to increase the amounts a little if you like your meat even juicier.

Pork roast (roughly 2 pounds)
1 medium onion, sliced
⅓ cup maple syrup
⅓ cup apple cider vinegar
1 teaspoon salt
1 teaspoon chili powder

> *Maple syrup (as well as birch, walnut, and others) makes an amazing meat marinade. Don't be afraid to experiment.*

1. Trim excess fat from the roast, if desired. Line the bottom of a slow cooker with onion slices, then place the roast on top.

2. Whisk together the maple syrup, apple cider vinegar, salt, and chili powder, and pour over the pork.

3. Cook on low for 8 hours, or until the meat is fall-apart tender.

4. Remove pork from slow cooker and place in a large bowl, reserving the cooking liquid. Shred gently with two forks. Toss with the cooking juices and serve on 6 large rolls (or 8 average-sized hamburger rolls).

MAKES 6–8 SANDWICHES

Mix Things Up

Always feel free to try a beloved recipe in a new way. My family likes using leftovers from the Nice-N-Slow Maple Chicken recipe on page 157 to make pulled chicken sandwiches on another day. Or use the Sloppy Maple Sandwiches recipe on page 161 as a starting point for Maple Calico Beans. Just add a variety of canned beans and bacon to the mix.

Relish the Real

IN TODAY'S OVER-SUGARED CULTURE, WE NEED A BETTER OPTION

I'll confess. I'm a maple-syrup-aholic. I slather my pancakes with our homemade syrup and bake with it and maple sugar with guilt-free abandon, but this was not always the case. I probably shouldn't mention this, but I'm going to come clean. I'm going to admit something that you probably won't relate to, since, well, you chose to read a book about how to make maple syrup. Here goes . . . I never liked rich, real maple syrup. I (gasp) preferred store-bought, fructose-laden, highly processed syrup in a bottle shaped like a sweet old lady. I can't explain this irrational behavior to you, now that I am oh-so-much wiser. I didn't see real syrup's value for the first four decades of my life.

Real food always trumps the alternatives

It was 100 percent Bill's idea to tap into the sugary joy running through the veins of the maples in our woods. I went along with the craziness just because it would be a great family project. The first few months, nothing changed my mind about maple syrup. Our eight measly jars of it were horribly dark, slightly crystalized, not-very-good-tasting, low-rate syrup, but when Bill experimented with a new product, when a few jars of syrup were crystalized beyond hope, and he (literally) whipped up some maple sugar, I

> **BILL'S TIP ON TAP**
> **Is maple syrup really just boiled maple tree sap? There's nothing else in it?**
>
> *Yep. This fact seems too good to be true, but it is. Syrup seems too sweet to have no additives, but it doesn't.*

Our first batch of maple sugar was dark, coarse, and imperfect, but delicious nonetheless.

was a convert. Now I was whole-heartedly "in" on this new family project. Folks say you want to use the best syrup to make the best maple sugar, but holy cow if that first batch of our maple sugar was "bad," well, I'll take "bad" maple sugar any day.

Then two things happened the following winter that turned my heart away from the dark side of not-real syrup forever. First of all, we talked to some experts and stopped "winging it" with our turning-sap-into-syrup efforts. As a result, we started churning out heavenly jars of golden liquid sugar. Secondly, I started reading about the goodness of real maple syrup. Until I became more knowledgeable myself, I didn't partake too much in our family's exuberance over maple syrup. In fact, I used it sparingly. I still thought the highly processed syrup on aisle 5 of my grocery store was somehow better for me. I was concerned that our homemade liquid sugary gold was too high in, well, sugar. What I wasn't thinking about was the difference in the sugar processed in a factory versus the sugar being created in nature—my own little wooded corner of nature, as a matter of fact.

Real food, gathered and packaged in real ways, will always trump any other alternative. Scientists have invested lots of lab time analyzing the properties of maple syrup, and the findings are incredible. While sugary foods aren't exactly revered for their health benefits, maple syrup may be the healthiest way to sweeten your food. Compare refined sugar, which is highly processed with zero nutrition, to maple syrup—an all-natural, totally real food—and maple syrup always wins. If used in moderation, it's truly a super food. Since maple syrup is also calorie dense, you do want to avoid overeating it, unless you enjoy weight gain. Since a high intake of any sugar can lead to dental decay, you do want to brush well after enjoying a syrupy treat, but as long as you eat it wisely, pure, all-natural, amazing maple syrup is, in my opinion, as good as a sweetener gets, y'all. I think the basic reason for that lies in the fact that we eat it in its natural state. In today's over-sugared culture, we need a truly healthy option.

MICHELLE'S TIP ON TAP
What about stevia? Is it as good a sweetener as maple sugar?

I actually used to use stevia a lot, because it is all-natural, but I greatly prefer the taste of maple, and it packs nutrients into every spoonful. Stevia carries zero calories, but it also carries zero nutrients.

Nutrition is complex

Back in 1988, when Oprah lost a ton of weight, she decided to make a memorable impression on her audience. She, consequently, changed our society's view of fat forever when she pulled a red Radio Flyer wagon onto the stage filled with nasty, greasy animal fat to represent how much weight she had lost. Seeing fat as the gross enemy in the 1980s and 1990s is, many experts believe, the root cause of America's obesity and diabetes crisis.

Real food has been around since the beginning, and it hasn't been proven wrong so far.

Then in 1992, the new food pyramid made the push for a low-fat diet official. It was obvious in the new pyramid that carbs were good and fat was bad. Indeed, that pyramid became the most widely adopted food guideline in the history of our nation. One survey reported that most Americans—more than 8 out of 10—believed the food pyramid was the basis of a perfect eating plan. The problem is that all of us who were the byproduct of that movement, myself included, wound up cutting out all fats, loving all carbs, and, ironically, facing obesity. Because not all fats are equal, some are even good, and not all carbs are equal. In fact, our body just converts the simple carbs (white bread and baked goods) into sugar.

The worst impact of the low-fat craze? It dramatically increased the amount of sugar that Americans were eating. You see, as a low-fat craze planted deep roots across the nation, the food industry developed thousands of low-fat options that resulted in high amounts of sugar and carbohydrates to make those foods taste good without the fat.

In the end, we eat 400 more calories today than we did before we watched Oprah pulling her disgusting wagon of animal fat, and we, as a nation, are facing an obesity epidemic. The best solution, in my mind, is to get back to eating more real food and real, all-natural sugar. The bottom line? Nutrition is complex! The science of nutrition is still young and evolving. But real food, the way God intended, well, it's been around since the beginning and it hasn't been proven wrong so far.

There's nothing refined about maple

When I learned a little about the production methods of refined sugar, and compared that process to our simple efforts making all-natural sugar, I began substituting maple syrup for refined sugar in baking and as an everyday sweetener whenever I could.

While maple syrup is made directly from boiled-down tree sap, straight from nature, with zero added any-thing, refined sugar is processed in a factory. It's made from either sugar cane or sugar beets and requires a huge amount of processing. First, the cane or beets are mixed with hot water. Then they're boiled and mashed to release the juices. Different chemicals are used at various points in the refining process. Then the cane or beet juices are filtered and whitened using carbon, bone char, or an ion exchange system. Once all the water eventually evaporates from the juice, the factory is left with the granulated, white sugar—99.96 percent sucrose—that gets shipped to your local grocery stores. The final product doesn't resemble the sweetener in its natural state at all at that point and it offers you zero health benefits, only pure sucrose.

Of course, the idea of maple syrup being a super-food sweetener is not a new one. The native people of Canada were making maple syrup—and gaining the health benefits

Raina Bailey, a reader in Colorado, is a huge maple syrup fan. While her family doesn't tap any trees, she explains that maple syrup is their sweetener of choice and it has changed the dynamics of her kitchen.

Raina's Dairy-Free Maple Soft Ice Cream

1 can full-fat coconut milk

3–4 cups frozen fruit

1 teaspoon vanilla

½ cup maple syrup

Blend the ingredients in a blender and eat immediately or freeze for an hour or so.

from it—long before European settlers had even heard of the idea of tapping a tree for sugar.

Maple syrup is a crazy, beneficial cocktail

Maple syrup and maple sugar contain an impressive list of compounds. In fact, science is discovering even more every year. For now, the minerals that we know are in maple include calcium, iron, magnesium, potassium, zinc, copper, and manganese. These minerals all play a part in important body functions, from cell formation to immune support, red blood cell maintenance to bone and teeth strength, and so much more. Maple syrup is also loaded with antioxidants, which boost our immune system. Maple syrup is swimming with polyphenolic compounds. In fact, maple syrup is truly a unique cocktail of crazy-beneficial compounds, combining some polyphenols you'll find in berries, some in tea, and some in flaxseed, but all in one teaspoon of maple syrup. By the way, I'm not making up this idea of a beneficial cocktail. If I counted the number of times I've read the word "cocktail" in reports and journals when scientists discuss the beneficial compounds in maple syrup, I might start to wonder if they write these reports during happy hour in the lab.

So, I've come to the conclusion that, as crazy as it seems, the sugar we collect, filter, and bottle straight out of a tree offers amazing, good-for-you stuff. I'm talking stuff like you find in fresh tomatoes, whole wheat, and red wine. This good stuff may protect our bodies from a slew of health problems—from cardiovascular disease to cancer and—this is where it gets really interesting—some of these compounds have not been found anywhere else.

I've read studies by Dr. Navidra Seeram, a professor in the Department of Biomedical and Pharmaceutical Sciences at the University of Rhode Island, and Dr. Nathalie Tufenkji, a professor in chemical engineering at McGill University in Quebec, Canada, and I'm blown away by the good stuff they've discovered in a spoonful of maple syrup. In fact, maple syrup has polyphenols that you won't find anywhere else in nature. When researchers in Japan fed mice some maple extracts with polyphenols, they found that gene expression was altered in the metabolism and the insulin sensitivity of the mice. Now I'm not even close to being a scientist, but I have to wonder if someday we might learn there's something in maple syrup that combats weight gain and high insulin levels. As implausible as that may sound—finding a compound in an all-natural sugar that fights diabetes—that's not even the scientific discovery about maple that gets me the most excited! (See page 177 to read about Dr. Nathalie Tufenkji's exciting research using maple syrup to combat bacteria.)

You can boil your sap and drink it too

Early on in my research to know more about maple, I had a nagging thought in the back of my mind. Doesn't boiling anything kill most of the good stuff in food? Like vegetables, for instance. I know I gain more nutritional benefit eating raw broccoli than cooked broccoli and more benefit eating fresh-picked green beans than canned ones. So wouldn't the same be true of maple?

Interestingly enough, the act of boiling actually makes more compounds in the sap. It seems that the combination of concentrating the sap into syrup, and heating the sap, causes the formation of unique compounds that no one has documented anywhere else in nature. So when we boil sap, we're doing chemistry in our backyards by introducing heat and making new compounds that you won't find anywhere else in anything else you eat. Now if that's not nutritional, delicious magic, well, I don't know what is. (Finally, I've found a chemistry class I can love, unlike high school chemistry. Sorry, Mrs. Smith, nothing against you.)

One such compound was found recently by researchers at the University of Rhode Island in Kingston. They were able to isolate a polyphenol that no one has ever seen before. As far as they can tell, it doesn't exist in the sap, only in maple syrup. One fun thing about being a scientist is you get to come up with cool names for things you discover. Since 80 percent of the world's syrup comes from Quebec, the researchers named this compound Quebecol. You've got to love that.

Fighting diabetes, germs, and inflammation

Scientists are wondering if Quebecol may be vital in the fight against type 2 diabetes and illnesses caused by bacteria. Quebecol has been found to be an effective anti-inflammatory. Even better—and so exciting!—Quebecol is being touted as a potential anti-cancer drug. Quebecol may someday be a more effective replacement for what's currently used in colon and breast cancer chemotherapy, with much less severe side effects. Even so, Quebecol is only one of the amazing ingredients you find in maple syrup.

Many scientists agree that the unique combination of antioxidants and anti-inflammatory properties in maple syrup may help fight chronic diseases.

Inulin is another newly discovered bonus in maple syrup. It's a complex carbohydrate, or a natural fiber, that is a sort of prebiotic. Amazingly enough, inulin works to encourage the growth of beneficial bacteria in our guts, joining forces with the other polyphenols, vitamins, and minerals that we already knew were housed in maple syrup. In fact, many scientists agree that the totally unique combination of antioxidants and anti-inflammatory properties in maple syrup very well may be discovered to aid in all kinds of chronic diseases, even neurodegenerative illnesses like Alzheimer's. Yep, research has shown that pure maple syrup can be linked to brain health. Honestly, I think it's about time for maple syrup to be used in kitchens around the world, don't you?

At a recent maple syrup symposium, where Dr. Navidra Seeram was one of the main organizers, he explained, "A healthy gut, with a balance of beneficial bacteria, helps to stimulate and support a healthy immune system. A healthy immune system, then, can help protect the body against chronic inflammation. Chronic inflammation has been shown to have a potential link to brain conditions such as Alzheimer's disease. As such, this research provides additional information linking pure maple syrup, a unique natural sweetener, to brain health."

On the flip side, while there are amazing compounds created when sap is boiled down to syrup, I'd be remiss if I didn't explain that some nutrition-rich ingredients are found in sap that no longer exist when the sap is boiled to syrup. Out of 10 antioxidant compounds found in sugar maple sap, only 3 are found in maple syrup. So, obviously at least 7 antioxidants are lost in the transformation from sap to syrup. So if you can drink maple sap and also use maple syrup and sugar as sweeteners, you're gaining a wide variety of different antioxidants and other compounds. Use sap in place of water to make drinks. Check out the end of this chapter for a few of my favorites.

So how can you add maple syrup to your day?

Any time you're using a sweetener, you can most likely make it maple. I love all forms of maple in my cup of hot tea. Some days I toss in a piece of hard maple candy, other days a chunk of maple sugar, and occasionally I'll go to the fridge for a teaspoon of maple syrup. It's easier to grab the sugar chunks or candies I always have handy in jars on the kitchen counter, so that's my go-to sweetener. If I want a little extra after I have a few sips, I've been known to sprinkle on a little extra maple sugar. I don't drink coffee, but I'm told maple coffee is wonderful too.

Maple syrup or sugar is wonderful drizzled or sprinkled on oatmeal or other hot cereals, fresh fruit, and cooked veggies, like baked squash. (See Dulce East's recipe, which calls for birch syrup but is also fantastic with maple syrup, on page 144.) Maple syrup is wonderful in marinades and can be substituted for honey in all homemade salad dressings. Of course it can be substituted for refined sugar in everything you bake.

MICHELLE'S TIP ON TAP
Is maple syrup a good sweetener for all kinds of beverages?
Because maple syrup is already a "simple" sugar, in liquid form, it easily dissolves in any beverages, making it a great all-natural sweetener for everything from lemonade to hot chocolate.

You can't go wrong with maple. Even when I mess up making soft candy, I get glorious sugar chunks that I love using in my tea.

How to use maple syrup in any recipe

Maple syrup is fantastic to bake with, as long as you know a few important basics. Just remember the three "R"s:

1. Replace 1 cup of sugar with ²⁄₃ to ³⁄₄ cup of maple syrup.

2. Remove about 3 tablespoons of liquid from the recipe.

3. Reduce your oven temperature by about 25°F, because maple syrup caramelizes at a lower temperature than refined sugar does. I've done the hard work and figured out these details for you for the recipes included in this book. You're welcome.

What do you need to know when you're buying your syrup?

Make sure you're purchasing 100 percent all-natural maple syrup. It's an added bonus if you can assure that your syrup was made by a single-source producer, which you can't do if you're grabbing your syrup off a big box store shelf or buying online, where one syrup bottle can be a mix of syrups from hundreds of different sugarmakers. (See the Resources section for more information.)

You might consider stocking up, or even buy in bulk, when you find syrup you love. You can keep unopened maple syrup in a cabinet or cool, dark place for a long time. Mine has been fine in my root cellar for years at a time. Once you've opened your syrup, however, you do want to make sure you keep it sealed tightly in the refrigerator, or mold will start to form on that sugary deliciousness.

Just how sweet is syrup?

A crazy thing happened a few years ago in San Francisco. A whole bunch of scientific-minded professionals put their heads together and shared their findings at a huge symposium focused entirely on (drum roll please) maple syrup. It was the first worldwide symposium to focus exclusively on the health benefits of that ambrosial yumminess we boil down from tree sap.

I've done some deciphering of the notes from the symposium and, honestly, maple syrup continues to impress the hand-knit socks off of me.

It's so impressive that I've weeded through the scientific jargon, talked to some experts, and boiled it down to some syrup adjectives you really need to know. According to these scientists, just look at all the things you can call this amber ambrosial sugar, in addition to delicious:

Antimicrobial. Maple syrup may offer a medical solution to the ever-growing problem of superbugs by improving the effectiveness of antibiotics—possibly as much as 90 percent! While this benefit doesn't help me when I'm slathering maple syrup on my pancakes, the fact that someday I may be able to take an antibiotic capsule, infused with maple extract, to ward off a bacterial infection is pretty exciting.

Antioxidant-rich. Science has known for a while that plant-based foods are the best sources for antioxidants, so of course, maple syrup (which comes directly from a maple tree) would be teeming with antioxidants. Some of the antioxidants in maple syrup are found nowhere else in nature.

Functional. Functional foods are foods that offer us more than just basic nutrition. A food has to have some other positive effect on our health for scientists to label it "functional." Take oatmeal. Because it's full of soluble fiber that helps lower cholesterol, it's a functional food. Other examples have to be modified to be "functional," like orange juice that has added calcium to improve bone health. For multiple reasons, and without any fortifying, pure maple is definitely a functional food. So when I choose to sweeten my drink or my cake or my meat glaze with all-natural maple syrup instead of refined sugar, I'm also adding essential vitamins and minerals to my diet that I'd never find in a refined sweetener.

Immune-boosting. Maple syrup is also full of polyphenols, which improve the body's ability to fight numerous health conditions, so maple boosts our immune system. When I'm feeling lousy or fighting off a cold, I need to add more sticky sweet maple to my day.

Prebiotic. Scientists discovered a complex carbohydrate, inulin, in maple syrup. Inulin is a natural fiber that works as a prebiotic. Maple syrup has carbohydrates that feed the good bacteria in my gut. Since the good bacteria pretty much call the shots in my intestines, maple syrup indirectly helps me digest nutrients, synthesize vitamins, manage my weight, make my bones stronger, fight against carcinogens, and keep my brain healthy.

Probiotic. Probiotics are live microorganisms that are good bacteria for our guts, and maple syrup has many. I've been fermenting my drinks (kombucha and switchel) and our family's been eating a lot more slow-fermented sourdough bread. You see, probiotics have a powerful impact on our overall digestive health, even reducing depression, improving skin, and promoting heart health. I love hearing that I can increase our probiotics by just switching our sweetener to maple.

Anti-diabetic. There are polyphenols in maple syrup that deter the way our bodies convert some carbohydrates to sugar. In fact, syrup is more effective at this than berries. Type 2 diabetes is still prevalent in our society, so finding a potential anti-diabetic compound in maple syrup is a pretty big deal. Not to mention that maple falls low on the glycemic scale. Basically, foods that fall low (55 or under) on this scale are better for us, even if we have no signs of diabetes. In fact, consuming foods that are lower on the glycemic index (and lower in carbohydrates) helps us prevent prediabetes. So where does maple fall? A sweet 54. Honey? 58. Refined sugar? 65. And, another bonus, maple contains fewer carbohydrates than the others as well.

Anti-inflammatory. Researchers have found special anti-inflammatory properties inside maple syrup. Umm, does this mean maple syrup is kind of like gooey delicious ibuprofen that I can pour on my pancakes?

Polyphenolic. I might have just made up a word, but you get the gist. The truth is that one little tablespoon of maple syrup has almost 20 mg of polyphenols. It just gets better every day, as ongoing research keeps finding more benefits to polyphenols. These micronutrients are essential to our overall health.

I'm not saying that adding maple syrup to your diet is a miracle cure to anything, but we all want some sweetness in our life, pretty much every day. Maple sweeteners give us an option that actually includes health benefits along with the sugar. Since the biggest influence we can have on our gut health is our diet, and since we are in total control of our diet, why not choose a sweetener that offers us health benefits? Bonus, why not choose a super-hero sweetener that may one day destroy superbugs, aid cancer patients, and save the lives of thousands of people a year who would otherwise die from a seemingly simple bacterium? (Keep reading for more on that.)

One Sweet Discovery

It's not every day that someone gets to talk to the Canada Research Chair in Biocolloids and Surfaces. So when Nathalie Tufenkji, who is on the cutting edge of fascinating research with (you guessed it) maple syrup, talked with me about her recent findings, I was honored.

Dr. Tufenkji heads up a research team in McGill's Department of Chemical Engineering that is discovering fascinating things about a few compounds in maple syrup that very well may revolutionize the way modern medicine fights superbugs. She's discovered that a concentrated cocktail of syrup extracts can do some major damage to nasty bacteria. Dr. Tufenkji's team has good cause to think that adding a simple cocktail of maple compounds directly into a capsule form of an antibiotic will greatly increase the success of it. This could potentially put an end to superbugs.

Yes, the syrup that you slather on your pancakes contains minute compounds that scientists could extract and use to kill bacteria.

I wondered if Dr. Tufenkji is as big a fan of maple in the kitchen as she is in the lab? "Absolutely! I love maple syrup," she told me. "But I really love maple cream. My favorite way to eat it is on toast." I knew there was a reason I liked this lady.

MAPLE SWITCHEL

I recently developed an infatuation for kombucha, a fermented drink that's a delicious way to improve your gut health. Maple switchel offers you fermented goodness and extra nutrients in an even simpler way. As a bonus, maple switchel is a caffeine-free, all-natural energy booster! I love making it with fresh maple sap.

½ **gallon water (or maple sap, if it's sugar season and you have a tree to tap)**
¾ **cup maple syrup**
4 **tablespoons grated ginger (about a 2-inch piece of ginger root)**
½ **cup apple cider vinegar**

1. Boil 2 cups of water, remove from heat, and steep the grated ginger in the pan for 20 minutes, covered.

2. For the best nutritional benefits, don't boil any other ingredients. Boiling destroys the living nutrients in the vinegar and the sap.

3. Strain out the ginger and mix in maple syrup and remaining water (or sap) as well as the apple cider vinegar. Enjoy at room temperature or chilled.

YIELDS 4 SERVINGS

MAPLE HOT CHOCOLATE

If you're looking for an all-natural alternative to soda or other sugary drinks for young ones around your table, using maple syrup has a lot of nutritional advantages. Nothing warms us up after collecting maple sap in the cold quite like a mug of maple hot chocolate.

¼ **cup unsweetened cocoa powder**

½ **teaspoon salt**

⅓ **cup water**

5 cups milk

⅓ **cup maple syrup**

1 teaspoon vanilla

1. Mix the dry ingredients in a saucepan.

2. Add the water and bring to a boil.

3. After a few minutes, add the milk and continue heating until it's the temperature you'd like to serve it.

4. Remove from heat. Stir in the maple syrup and vanilla, and serve.

YIELDS 2–3 SERVINGS

MAPLE LEMONADE

Want to know how I make the best fresh-squeezed lemonade ever? I substitute maple syrup for sugar. The result is a beautiful blend of true, all-natural, deeply-sweet maple and fresh, tart, pulp-filled lemon.

2 cups freshly squeezed lemon juice
¾ cup maple syrup
5 cups water

Mix the three ingredients together and serve chilled, over ice. Or, if you happen to make this during sugaring season and you have maple sap nearby, use sap instead of water for an added "wow" and extra antioxidants.

YIELDS 2 QUARTS

Shake or Slather It On

WARNING: READING THIS CHAPTER WILL RESULT IN A NEW OBSESSION

Okay, you immediately know what to do with maple syrup when there's a stack of warm pancakes in front of you, but what about maple sugar? If you're like most people, you don't really know what to make of it. I mean, you certainly wouldn't pour a jar of it over your breakfast plate.

In this chapter, I'm not only going to fill you in on the amazingness of this all-natural granulated yumminess, but also will explain why it's the best sweetener ever—in my completely unprofessional but totally taste-bud-oriented opinion. By the time you've finished reading this chapter, you'll have many ideas of exactly what you want to do with maple sugar, and you might not want to wait one more day to get your hands on some. Which is okay, because you'll also be able to make some in your own kitchen. Seriously. I take no responsibility for the obsession that results thereafter.

It's an age-old obsession

Yes, I'm a maple addict (but you already knew this). If I had to choose just one form of maple sweetener, I'd choose maple sugar. Of course, I'm not the first

> **MICHELLE'S TIP ON TAP**
> **Should I buy organic maple syrup?**
>
> *Truth is, all maple syrup is 100 percent sap, with the water removed. That's organic whether you have a special sticker on it or not. Sugarhouses that go the extra mile to earn that sticker do jump through hoops. They practice forest management practices, use special defoamers, and follow specific requirements of different agencies. Purchasing organic syrup supports hard-working sugarmakers who go to extremes to provide the best product they can. The call is yours.*

one to encourage an obsession for maple sugar. Robert Beverley, a Virginian historian in 1705, described maple sugar as "bright and moist, with a large full grain." Johann Kohl, a German living among an Ojibwa tribe near Lake Superior in 1858, wrote about a neat way the Ojibwa preserved their maple sugar: "they pour it, just before crystallization, into wooden molds, in which it becomes nearly hard as stone. They make it into all sorts of shapes, bear's paws, flowers, stars, small animals, and other figures, just like our gingerbread-bakers at fairs. This sort is principally employed in making presents." But I personally like the way Native Americans described maple sugar to Kohl. They told him it "tastes fragrant—more of the forest."

A hundred years earlier, in 1751, Peter Kalm, a Swedish botanist who wrote about his experiences with early French fur traders and northern Native American tribes, described how the native people, "long before the Europeans discovered America, made maple sugar. The Europeans have now learned the method and nearly all of them who live where this tree grows make a large quantity of sugar each year." He also noted that "if sugar in a special form is desired, the thick syrup can be . . . poured into shells or other vessels, depending on the shape desired, and allowed to cool."

While it's not a new thing, making maple sugar is new to many people, so you may be surprised just how easy it is. Four things you probably don't know about maple sugar:

1. Maple sugar was probably first made by Native Americans in the United States and Canada.

2. Maple sugar was the Native Americans' preferred product to make with maple sap, because it's the most practical maple product to store (since maple syrup requires canning, and maple cream requires refrigeration).

3. Maple sugar was a common sweetener until the turn of the twentieth century, when suddenly cane sugar became less expensive than maple sugar.

4. Maple sugar, when purchased from a small sugar farm, helps sustain a valuable growing process and support a farming family.

Why maple sugar is my favorite granulated sweetener

If we could make enough maple sugar to use it as our sole sweetener on our homestead, I'd be all in. As it is, I buy maple syrup before the year is over, but that doesn't stop me

I use Mom's old Mason jars to hold important kitchen necessities. Maple sugar is always the first in line.

from making sure we always have some maple sugar and candies on hand. In fact, I have a row of Mason jars that hold staples on my kitchen counter, from rice to popcorn kernels to maple candy. My Grandmom Rosie Kasecamp and my Uncle Thurman both taught me well. I never visited Rosie's kitchen without having a pink wintergreen lozenge, brought down from the ledge over the wood cooking stove. I never passed through Thurman's kitchen, en route to the back door, without a candy root beer barrel, wrapped in brown cellophane, fished out of a bowl sitting on the counter. I love it that I can have a jar of all-natural maple candies—made from our own trees—always sitting on mine.

In my row of jars, maple sugar is the first in line, always at the ready to sweeten a cup of tea or sprinkle on some yogurt. As a bonus, we have found that maple sugar is a great thing to make with homemade syrup that's a little too dark or crystallized.

Here are just a few reasons that maple sugar holds the premier spot on my list of favorite sweeteners:

- It creates a warm sweetness when used in baking.
- It has fewer calories than refined sugar. (Now that's sweet!)
- It has a low glycemic index, meaning it may be a sweetener that diabetics can use, in moderation.
- It is loaded with antioxidants that support the body's immune system.
- It supports heart health.
- It is loaded with beneficial vitamins and minerals.

Now that I've introduced you to maple sugar's tasty benefits, you may wonder if you can truly make it yourself. Not only is the answer a whole-hearted "yes," but making maple sugar doesn't even require tapping trees. You can make maple sugar from purchased maple syrup. Read on. You can thank me later.

Put your maple sugar where your oven is

Of course, the Native Americans had it right. Sugar is easier to store, and even use, than liquid syrup. You definitely can use maple syrup in baking, but maple sugar provides all the flavor of maple syrup without requiring you to do any converting of ingredients. When you consider that maple sugar is totally shelf stable, indefinitely, you know you're on to something great. You can use it as a replacement for both refined white sugar and light and dark brown sugars in your baking, for different, all-natural options. No wonder it's becoming quite a luxury item in natural-food and health-food stores as a healthy alternative to processed, refined beet and cane sugars.

In addition to the recipes found in this chapter, here are several quick ways to use maple sugar:

- Use maple sugar in waffle and pancake recipes.
- Replace refined sugar with maple sugar in apple pie and apple crisp.
- Sprinkle it on your warm, buttered pancakes or French toast.
- Shake some over your bowl of warm oatmeal.

- Adorn cupcakes with maple sugar in place of sprinkles.
- Turn your next bowl of vanilla ice cream into a little bit of maple heaven.
- Create a yummy maple sugar glaze, or a BBQ sauce, for ham or pork.
- Drizzle canola oil over fresh-popped popcorn, then shake some maple sugar, a touch of cinnamon, and some salt over your healthy snack.
- Sweeten plain yogurt with maple sugar.
- Liven up fresh fruit by shaking a little maple sugar on top.
- Sprinkle maple sugar on toast as you would cinnamon sugar.
- Sprinkle maple sugar on bacon as soon as it's done cooking. (Nate Blakeslee, a sugarmaker in Panama, New York, taught me this trick. The sugar absorbs into the meat and makes for the most amazing bacon you've ever had.)
- Rub some into your meat, like Douglas Bramow, a maple enthusiast in Cedar Rapids, Iowa, does before he puts it in his smoker. You'll savor the extra flavor.
- And, my favorite, add a spoonful of maple sugar to your cup of hot tea.

Whether you make it or buy it, bake with it, shake it on, or stir it in, maple sugar is an amazingly delicious, healthy alternative that your family will love.

Make your own maple sugar

Believe it or not, you can actually make this marvelous sweetener right in your own kitchen. Today. You just need some genuine maple syrup, a quality mixer, a candy thermometer, and lots of patience. I've never thought to closely measure my input and output. I guess I'm always too busy drooling with anticipation to be levelheaded. The folks who publish the Cornell Maple Bulletin, unlike me, are scientific and detail-oriented. They report that a quart of syrup will yield about 2 pounds of maple sugar. By the way, I should take a second to save the lives of kitchen mixers across the country. If you don't have a professional-grade mixer, grab a few able-bodied family members to take turns with the spoon, and do this by hand. It will take a while, but you really have to trust a lady whose husband thought any old mixer was fine. After our regular-ole mixer died while mixing a batch of maple sugar, we purchased a commercial one that I've loved using for years now.

BIG IDEAS AND LOTS OF SYRUP

Hayley's not a diminutive kind of girl, never has been. Her birth weight set records at 11.5 pounds. She's had big ideas ever since. When Hayley learned about the healing impact of art, she got her sisters and mentors in the Philly non-profit group, TechGirlz to assemble and deliver mini art kits to children's hospitals. She and her sisters were named Governor Volunteers of the Year. When we moved to rural New England, she discovered how much she loved to capture her new life with photography and writing. She's been blogging and running occasional TechGirlz workshops ever since, all while doing morning and evening farm chores of course.

Hayley loves a homestead morning. Scout's warm udders. Selah's quiet stirring in her stall. The rhythmic spray of the milk hitting the steel pail.

Then, after pouring fresh milk from the pail into ½-gallon jars, Hayley occasionally—on the best mornings—makes maple cinnamon rolls for breakfast.

Hayley wants to be an author or a professional videographer. "My growing-up years on a small New England farm—days that were filled with simple details—will always influence everything I create," she says.

Hayley's favorite thing to do with maple?

"I love to slather it all over my breakfast plate. No reason to limit it just to pancakes."

Depending on your grade of syrup, it will have slightly different amounts of invert sugars, which is the deciding factor on how light or dark, fine or coarse, your sugar turns out. I personally love all the variety and have never made a maple sugar I didn't love. In general, if you are shooting for a fine-grained sugar, the mid-season syrup might prove most productive for you. The late-season (usually darker) syrup might prove better for maple cream and candies.

Step 1. Heat

First, heat the syrup to 253°F. Well, actually the temperature depends on your altitude. Officially, you'll need to heat the syrup to 41°F above the boiling point of water where you live. Of course, the quality of your thermometer is also a factor. To gauge both your boiling point where you live as well as the quality of your thermometer, you can simply bring a pot of water to boil with the thermometer you'll be using to make your maple sugar. Note what your thermometer reads when the water begins to boil. Add 41°F to that amount, and you will know the perfect temperature for removing your syrup from the stove when making sugar.

BILL'S TIP ON TAP

Why is each batch of syrup such a different color?

Sap is made up of water, sugar, minerals, and other organic compounds (such as proteins and vitamins). At different points of the season, in different trees, in different parts of the country, the exact makeup of those minerals and compounds varies, which means the taste and color will vary. Typically, early sap makes very light, delicately flavored syrup, while later sap makes darker colored, robust flavored syrup.

MICHELLE'S TIP ON TAP

I've heard light syrup makes better sugar. Is this true?

While professional sugar houses always use their golden colored syrup when making maple sugar, I personally love the gorgeous variety of colors, textures, and tastes I create when I use all different colors of syrups. The lighter syrup is made in the early days of the maple season, and it makes very fine, light colored maple sugar. As the weather warms and leaf buds begin to swell, the chemistry of the sap changes, and the clear liquid darkens slightly. Late-season syrup is darker in color and richer in taste, making a larger-grained, darker maple sugar.

Depending on your grade of syrup, it will have slightly different amounts of invert sugars, which is the deciding factor on how light or dark, fine or coarse, your sugar turns out.

Calibrating your thermometer

Whenever you need to gauge a very specific temperature of boiling syrup, either to bottle it or to turn it into sugar or candy, it's a great idea to calibrate your thermometer. Not only does your altitude impact the boiling point, but so can the weather, which, in turn, impacts every one of the recipes you'll follow for making any maple confection. (A typical high or low pressure change can alter the boiling point as much as two degrees.) To calibrate your thermometer, simply bring a pot of water to boil with the thermometer in the water. Note what your thermometer reads when the water begins to boil. If it's anything different than 212°F, you'll need to alter the temperatures on the chart on page 198 accordingly.

Once the syrup reaches that magic temperature (for us, it's 253°F), remove the pan from the heat and pour the now-darker-and-thicker syrup into your mixer's bowl. You can let the syrup cool down some if you'd like (but no lower than 200°F) before you start mixing it.

Step 2. Mix

Making maple sugar does require a lot of mixing. And mixing. And then more mixing. Stirring aggressively tends to make a finer, more powdery sugar, while slow, even stirring tends to make a grainier sugar, which can sometimes turn out similar to common brown sugar. But I've got to be real here: The look and taste of our sugar varies greatly from one attempt to the next, and I'm good with that. The picture on page 192 of two distinctly different maple sugars gives you an idea of what I'm talking about. Those are two different batches of sugar from two distinctly different batches of homemade syrup. We made the darker, coarser sugar (in the bowl) from a batch of maple syrup that we boiled down too long, so it was dark and crystallized. We made the lighter color, finer sugar (in the blue jar) from much lighter syrup, which maybe should have boiled down just a little bit longer when we originally made the syrup. Both are delicious, just different.

As the heated syrup starts turning to granulated sugar (trust me, it will happen, magically), your almost-sugar may rise up in volume. If you need to, turn off the mixer, and the volume will decrease again. Be sure to keep mixing the sugar until all moisture has been beaten out of it (that's extra important) and the sugar is finely granulated.

The most magical part of the whole process is when a large "poof" suddenly rises out of your mixing bowl. It reminds me of an old cartoon when a large cloud of smoke quickly pops out of a witch's cauldron. Turns out this happens because the crystallization process releases a good amount of heat. The poof you see is a sudden release of hot steam. I bet you didn't know you'd have a mini chemistry lesson here, did you? This poof of steam has never been significant for us, but I've been told it can be a pretty large burst and could actually cause burns, so do use caution. You may even want to pull out those old chem lab goggles if you happen to have a pair.

Step 3: Sift

For our batch of maple syrup that was over boiled, dark, and crystallized, we discovered that using it to make maple sugar was a great choice. It did make very large granules of sugar that we worked through a sieve to make finer sugar. But we kept some in the larger size too. We actually like having a variety of maple sugars on hand—from ultra-fine to large granules. We love the larger granules for sprinkling on ice cream and cupcakes or using in a morning cup of hot tea or evening cup of hot cocoa, to start and end the day with a burst of natural sweetness.

> *Want powdered maple sugar? Simply place some maple sugar in a blender until it's the fine powder that you're looking for.*

We always have the wood stove and fireplace cranking when we make and package our maple sugar, so we don't have much concern about humidity causing our sugar to clump up. It's a good idea to try to package your sugar in a humidity-controlled room and sift your sugar a minimum of two times before packing it away in jars, plastic storage containers, or zipped bags. Both of these factors will help reduce the likelihood that your sugar clumps up.

Step 4: Test your maple sugar

There is a pretty foolproof way to check if your moisture is good when you're packaging your maple sugar. It's called "the creep test," and while it sounds like a great way to filter out your daughter's bad boyfriends, it really works for sugar.

To conduct this "creep test," you simply make a tiny pile of maple sugar on a clean, dry surface. Then pour additional maple sugar on top. Sugar that is still too wet will not creep, but it will cling together at this point. Sugar that is too dry doesn't creep either; it will just slide down. Good creeping begins to occur about the time the pile is an inch high. You will see the sugar begin to move down the slope. It creeps or moves with a thick fluid motion that makes it appear as though it's crawling. In fact, it almost looks like it's alive. If your sugar creeps well, it's ready to package.

If you forget to try the creep test and wind up packaging your maple sugar when it's moist, it will harden into solid blobs. If that happens, all is not lost. You could try to break up the clumps of sugar in a blender. You can also let it stand overnight in a sealed jar with a damp paper towel. Sometimes that loosens it up. Or, for a quick fix, heat the needed amount in a 250°F oven for a few minutes, or in a microwave on low for 1–2 minutes per cup. The negative? If you do wind up having to soften your maple sugar in the oven, you should use it immediately. Or maybe that's not so much of a negative.

The absolute perfect reason to love maple sugar

It turns out, not only can you make maple sugar from maple syrup, but if you have maple sugar you can make maple syrup! I mean seriously. You can store maple sugar indefinitely. Like forever, folks. So if you know this trick you can stockpile your sugar and turn it into syrup whenever you want. As my mom would say, "Now how about them apples!?"

Add 7 tablespoons of water to one cup of packed maple sugar. Heat and stir continually until all the sugar is dissolved in the solution and voila! You have syrup again. Want to do more? Add just a little under a cup of water to 2 packed cups of maple sugar. Want do a single serving? Add 1 tablespoon of water to 2 heaping tablespoons of

MICHELLE'S TIP ON TAP
Can I bake with maple sugar in place of white sugar?

Baking with maple sugar is even easier than baking with maple syrup. You can substitute maple sugar for refined sugar in any recipe in a 1:1 ratio. No other change is necessary.

tip

Sweet Drinks

Your tea-loving friends will thank you for this. Once you've perfected your maple sugar making abilities (which pretty much just takes one attempt) you can make this gift for someone special. Just grind up milk chocolate chips and white chocolate chips with some maple sugar, place them in a pretty jelly jar, and add a label. I like to include directions: "Add 1–3 teaspoons to a cup of your favorite hot tea, hot chocolate, or coffee." While you're at it, whip up a few batches for your own pantry so you can make a delicious warm drink whenever you're craving maple, or chocolate, or both.

Maple double chocolate sweetener makes a sweet gift.

maple sugar. Of course you can make the syrup thicker by adding less water. There is one caution though; you'll want to use this syrup pretty soon after you make it. If you set it in your fridge for a few days, you'll most likely find it's recrystallized.

With so many wonderful reasons and ways to use maple sugar, you probably don't need any more convincing that your kitchen needs to always have some of this goodness around. If you do, try out some maple cinnamon rolls on page 207.

Maple Cream

Maple cream is one of my favorite maple products we make on our homestead. But right up front, I think we need to talk about what we want to call this yumminess. A quick online search indicates that a lot of people call this wonderful, creamy sweetness "maple butter." I have qualms with this moniker. Whenever I hear someone call it that I immediately think of apple butter. Apple butter was a prominent staple of my youth, and I never cared for it. So I never want to lump apple butter and glorious maple cream together in my brain. This thick but spreadable 100 percent pure all-maple wonder can be used on toast, crackers, pretzels, bagels, muffins, pancakes, waffles, doughnuts, shortbread cookies, or any ole thing your heart desires. While it sounds so very decadent, there is a huge bonus to maple cream over so many other things you might be

tempted to slather on your toast. Maple cream is an all-natural product. Even though it's sugar, it contains important nutrients such as amino acids, proteins, organic acids, minerals (calcium and potassium being the most prevalent) and even trace levels of some vitamins. Crazy enough, it even contains antioxidants. Now that's a lot better than the high fructose corn syrup, hydrogenated vegetable oil, or dextrose you'll find in store-bought jellies or that peanut butter that supposedly choosy mothers choose. (By the way, don't miss the recipe at the end of this chapter for a far superior choice of peanut butter.)

Maple cream—everything it touches becomes heavenly.

SWEET SUGGESTIONS FROM A SUGARMAKER

Bette Lambert has no memory of a winter without maple. She does remember excitedly gathering sap buckets as soon as she could walk at the Vermont sugaring operation her parents opened in the 1940s. Bette is now the head of product development and marketing and her son, Paul, is the head of production. The sugarhouse? It's Paul's design, and it runs completely on the sun's power.

Bette's advice?

All new sugarmakers should go to experienced sugarmakers for advice and encouragement. "We're all eager to help," she says.

Bette's equipment recommendation?

Bette suggests that every backyard sugarmaker try their hand at maple cream, maple sugar, and super-easy sugar on snow. While these can be made with just a pint of syrup and a wooden spoon, a heavy-duty stand mixer is worth its weight in gold for making maple sugar.

Bette's favorite recipe?

Bette Lambert loves working in the sugarbush today as much as she did when she was a kid.

Baked Beans in Maple

1. Soak two cups of dried soldier beans overnight.

2. Rinse off and add enough water to cover the beans. Boil them until the skins of the beans crack when blown on.

3. Drain and then make syrup with 2 cups dark maple syrup, ½ teaspoon ginger, ¼ teaspoon black pepper, 1 teaspoon dry mustard, and 2 teaspoons salt.

4. Slice one onion and place in the bottom of a bean pot or casserole dish. Alternate beans with syrup, then add enough water to fill pot. If desired, slice ¼ pound of salt pork and place on top of beans.

5. Cover and bake at 300°F for 6–8 hours. Check occasionally and add more water if necessary to keep beans from drying out.

So, in my limited chemistry-minded way, I'll explain how this creamy magic happens because it's pretty fascinating, yet so simple at the same time. To make maple sugar, cream, or candies, you have to start with some supersaturated syrup. The exact temperature of the syrup, how you stir (or don't stir) the syrup, and how you cool the syrup all have an impact on what you wind up with. All of these factors impact the size of the crystals that form in your concoction.

As you heat it to make sugar or cream, the syrup becomes viscous and, if left alone, will start to solidify (think hard candy) before crystals can form and grow. On the other hand, if that hot, supersaturated syrup is stirred while it's cooling, it will form crystals. I'm told that the mechanical motion of the spoon causes microscopic crystal nuclei to form (or something like that). Basically, if you keep stirring, you form crystals, mix those tiny crystals throughout the thickened syrup, and cause them to grow in size and increase in number. Depending on what you want to make, you'll need different sizes of

TEMPERATURE CHART FOR MAKING MAPLE SUGAR, CREAM, AND CANDIES

Type	Temperature to heat syrup to	Cooling instructions	Directions
Maple sugar	253°F	Cool to 200°F, or you can skip the cooling time	Stir vigorously until you have sugar.
Molded maple sugar	253°F	Do not cool	Stir hot syrup just until crystals form, then pack it into molds to harden. Since these are packed, not poured, these won't be ultra pretty candies. For that, you want to try soft candy, below.
Maple cream	234°F	Cool rapidly to 100°F	Stir slowly with a wooden spoon, until you have cream.
Soft candy	244°F	Let cool to 175°F	Beat with wooden spoon until it's turned a nice cream color. Then pour it into greased molds. If you stir it just a minute too long you will have something too thick to pour into molds. These candies will have a pretty glazed look to them, unlike the molded maple sugar.
Hard candy	300°F	Do not cool	Immediately pull from heat and very carefully pour into lightly greased molds (or cookie tray).

*For all maple confections, lighter, early season syrup and mid-season syrup will be the easiest to turn into sugar, cream, and candies. Late season syrup tends not to crystalize as well.

After filling every candy mold we own, we will smooth out our remaining hard candy on greased cookie trays to cool. We seem to always have already hardening candy before the spreading is even done.

Even when maple products turn out not so pretty, like these rejected pieces of soft and hard candy, they are always oh-so yummy.

crystals. Thankfully other folks have figured out all the details. So right here, with zero knowledge of the chemistry of maple syrup, I can break it all down for you and have you making the best maple cream and candies ever. You will find a slight range of temperatures works okay for most of these confections, but I'm listing the details that have proven to work the best for me.

> **Make some sugar on snow!**
> *Boil a little syrup to 235°F then immediately drizzle it on packed snow. It hardens on contact. That's seriously all there is to making this yumminess.*

Also, the temperatures listed are assuming you're at a standard altitude and the boiling point of water where you are is at 212°F. If not, see page 192 for details on calibrating your thermometer. I should also warn you—it's kind of obvious, but still—that to make any of these glorious confections, you will be working with some really hot syrup, folks, so do use caution.

The nitty gritty on making maple cream

You will need to use 100 percent real maple syrup to make maple cream. If you have syrup you've tapped yourself, even better.

Heat the pure maple syrup to 234°F, or 22°F above the boiling point of water. (For more details, see "Calibrating your thermometer" on page 192.) Be sure to use a pot that is at least twice the size of the volume of your syrup because it will bubble and rise a lot. You can expect it to take a while (maybe 15–20 minutes) to reach 234°F. *The New York State Convections Notebook*, published by the Cornell Maple Program, suggests that you boil to a few degrees higher on rainy or humid days.

Top: Monitor your syrup closely as it boils away, until it reaches the magic temperature.

Bottom left: Once it's the correct temperature, immediately remove your pan from the heat and place it directly on ice, in a prepared bowl.

Bottom center: After stirring for about 10–15 minutes, you'll be close to done.

Bottom right: As you stir, you'll notice your contents getting lighter in color and thicker in consistency, until suddenly you've made maple cream.

As soon as the thermometer reaches that magic number, immediately remove the pot from the heat and place it directly on ice, in a bowl you have already prepared. Let it sit, undisturbed, until the contents cool to 100°F. Then you need to enlist some help and get busy stirring. If at this point some cooled syrup has hardened to the interior of the pot, dip the pan into hot

> **MICHELLE'S TIP ON TAP**
> **Are products like maple cream and maple candies higher in calories when they're made from darker syrup?**
>
> *Though syrups vary greatly in color, all grades of pure maple syrup are defined by their Brix (see page 90) and are all identical in density and sugar content.*

water for a few seconds and it should loosen up. Now you have about 15 minutes' worth of stirring ahead of you, so we like to rely on many hands to take part in the stirring. The good news is it's not overly strenuous. Instead, you want to stir slowly without beating or whipping the syrup. You'll notice the contents of your pot will get more fluid before they start to stiffen. Then they'll get lighter in color and thicker in consistency as you stir, until suddenly you realize you've done it. You've created heavenly delicious maple cream. Now spread it on something sweet or something salty, slather it on a warm bagel, or coat a strawberry in it, and enjoy. While maple cream is a little more difficult to make than a tray of soft candy, you can't slather your warm bagel with a piece of candy.

You will want to store your cream in the refrigerator, but don't be surprised if after a day it looks different. Are you familiar with those all-natural, top-grade peanut butters with natural oils that sit on the top of the jar until you stir them in? This attribute assures you it's different than the highly-processed, cheap brands, right? Well, maple cream is also an all-natural, top-grade product, and a small amount of the syrup will separate out and lay on the top of the cream in your jar. I can't tell you the chemistry behind that, although I'm sure it's a simple phenomenon, but I can tell you it doesn't impact the deliciousness one tiny bit. It does leave you with a choice, though. You can choose to either skim off that separated syrup and pour it in your morning cup of tea, or mix it right back into the cream before you slather it on your bagel. Don't you just love those kinds of choices?

And speaking of peanut butter, you haven't really tasted any at all until you whip up some of your own maple peanut butter.

MAPLE PEANUT BUTTER

Homemade, all-natural, super-easy Maple Peanut Butter. Oh my goodness, it doesn't get any more amazing than this in my kitchen, y'all! You definitely want to make this.

3 cups (16 oz) salted and shelled peanuts
3 tablespoons maple syrup

1. Preheat oven to 250°F.
2. Seriously. You need only two ingredients. Roast peanuts on a cookie tray in the oven for 20 minutes. Simply spread the peanuts in a single layer on a cookie sheet and bake on a middle rack of the oven.
3. Immediately, while the peanuts are still warm, use a food processor to cream them. It may take quite a few minutes to get a creamy consistency, but don't give up. Also, if your food processor is extra large (like mine), you will want to double this recipe. The nuts need to fill up a large portion of your bowl for the processor to cream them well.
4. Once you have a creamy peanut butter, add 1 tablespoon of maple syrup for every 1 cup of peanuts that you started with and mix it in.
5. Store in an airtight container at room temperature for several weeks. At least I think that's how long it will last, but I haven't been able to test this theory because this stuff is always gone in a heartbeat in my house (and half a heartbeat if I decide to share it with my family).

YIELDS 2 CUPS

MAPLE POPCORN

When Bill and I were newlyweds, staying in my cousin's little condo a few blocks from the Ocean City boardwalk in Maryland, our obsession began. A little shop that specialized in caramel popcorn became our favorite stop that weekend. I soon learned to make homemade caramel popcorn that rivaled the shop's, but our obsession deepened when I discovered I could make a version with all-natural maple syrup. Jackpot!

12 quarts popped popcorn*
2 cups butter
4½ cups packed brown sugar (or maple sugar)
½ cup maple syrup
½ cup molasses (or I like to use all-natural sorghum syrup)

1. Preheat oven to 250°F.

2. Divide your popped popcorn among four or five large bowls. If possible, have a few sets of willing hands on call to help. (Be sure to sift through the popcorn and remove any unpopped kernels to avoid a cracked tooth!)

3. Bring the other ingredients to a boil over medium heat, and then keep the pan at a medium boil for 5 minutes, stirring constantly. Remove from heat and quickly pour the syrup and sugar topping evenly over the bowls of popcorn, and stir each one, being sure to evenly coat all the popcorn with the maple topping before it starts to cool. (This is where helpers come in really handy.)

4. Spread the coated popcorn (whatever is left after your helpers devour some of it while they stir) onto two roasting pans, and bake for 1 hour. Break it apart while it's still warm, right out of the oven, and store for two or three days in an airtight container.

YIELDS 12 QUARTS

* We love using our air-popper when we make our Maple Popcorn. We find it takes about 1½ cups of kernels to make 12 quarts of popped popcorn.

DRIZZLED MAPLE POPCORN

When we're craving legit, intense caramel popcorn, we make the recipe on page 205. But if the movie is waiting and my energy is waning, this is my go-to special treat.

Freshly popped popcorn (about 8–10 cups)
1 tablespoon butter
⅓ cup maple syrup
1 teaspoon vanilla

1. First get your popcorn ready in an extra-large bowl. I find I need about ½ cup of kernels to make 10 cups of air-popped popcorn.

2. Melt together, on the stovetop, the butter and syrup. Remove from heat, stir in the vanilla, and immediately drizzle it over your popcorn.

3. Stir your popcorn well, making sure to incorporate every bit of topping that may pool in the bottom of your bowl. Add salt if you'd like a caramel taste, or go salt-free for a sweeter, more maple taste. Your popcorn won't be totally coated, like the maple popcorn (if it were, it would be too soggy), but it will be pleasantly sweet.

YIELDS 8–10 CUPS

MAPLE CINNAMON ROLLS

Ever since baking cinnamon rolls with a college friend, I've been hooked. Melissa started the obsession long ago. Now that I've added maple, this addiction is for life.

For the rolls:
About 2 cups flour
¼ cup sugar
2¼ teaspoons yeast (or one packet)
½ teaspoon salt
½ cup warm milk
3 tablespoons oil
1 egg

For the filling:
2 tablespoons soft butter (to spread on the rolled-out dough)
¼ cup brown sugar (or maple sugar)
2 teaspoons ground cinnamon

For the maple frosting:
¾ cup butter
⅛ cup maple syrup
1½ tablespoons heavy cream
1½ cups confectioner's sugar

1. Preheat oven to 350°F.
2. Place 1½ cups of the flour into a mixer along with the sugar, yeast, and salt. Add the warm milk, and mix slightly.
3. Add the oil and the egg. Mix for three minutes on medium-high. Add more flour, as needed, until the dough forms a tacky and soft, but still manageable, dough. Knead for five minutes, then cover it and let it rest for 10 minutes, at room temperature.

4. Melt the ¾ cup butter on the stove in a light-bottomed sauce pan and add in the maple syrup. (The light bottom will help you tell when the butter has browned.) Let the butter/maple combination simmer about 8–10 minutes, stirring often, then place the browned butter in the fridge.

5. Roll the dough out into a large rectangle, then spread the 2 tablespoons soft butter over the top. Mix the brown sugar (or maple sugar) and cinnamon together and sprinkle the mixture evenly over the whole rectangle, on top of the butter.

6. Gently roll the dough up into a tube. Cut the roll into 8–9 rounds, and place them in a pie pan. Cover them with a thin dish towel and allow them to rise until they're about double in size and quite puffy. Bake them for 15 minutes, or until the tops are golden.

7. Once the browned butter is cool/firm in the fridge, remove it and whip it until it's fluffier. Add in the heavy cream and confectioner's sugar and whip until the frosting is thick, perfect for spreading over your rolls.

YIELDS 8 ROLLS

Afterword

The winter before I started writing this book was a messy, difficult season. Summer had been oh-so-good. Mom and Dad had visited for a few weeks. Dad collected fresh eggs, watered the garden, and tended to the animals with me most days. Mom broke green beans with Jordyn and canned blueberry jam with Kayla and me. Together, we talked of pie for dessert and laughed as we collected bowls of mulberries, shaking the branches

and watching the ripe berries drop and cover the old sheets and drop cloths we had laid on the ground under the tree. Dad's height was advantageous, but his lack of balance had him teetering on the slope in front of our house, where the mulberry tree was planted long ago.

Three short months later I was in a panic, hopping on the next flight out of Boston to be my mother's advocate in her valiant battle against the swift, decisive destructiveness of chemotherapy. I treasure that I could spend a month by her side, daily, as I realized I was slowly saying goodbye. I also treasure that I could spend another month with my daddy, he and I grieving the loss of the most treasured lady in our life, together, as we moved him here to our farm. We spent December nights around a warm fire, loving Dad's childhood stories with a depth we hadn't before, and longing for May afternoons of gathering eggs and tending to the garden with him. His heart couldn't handle the separation from his girl of 55 years, and God decided he didn't need to anymore. On

New Year's Eve, Dad's heart made its last effort, and I suddenly felt I was facing a new year totally empty and utterly alone.

I realize, now that they're gone, how tightly my parents are woven into my own fiber. Each habit, mannerism, and thought of mine that mimics one of theirs still occasionally leaves an empty feeling where the thread weaves through my days. But the void is modest, and God graciously sews blessings into the gaps. The process of writing this book became cathartic for me and was indeed a monumental one of those blessings.

A few short months after I had chosen hymns and flowers for my parents' funerals and my brother and I had packed up our childhood memories, full sap buckets lined our farmhouse porch, and the smell of maple cooking on the stove silently breezed through the rooms. With the promise of spring ahead, hope arrived in the form of a seemingly successful surgery that eased our sweet daughter's years of chronic pain.

Then, sadly, despair creeped in and loomed over our summer when Jordyn faced a diagnosis of a rare neurological syndrome resulting from nerve damage during her spinal surgery that she didn't realize until the nerves started to try to heal many weeks after surgery. My unexpected loss of both parents, only weeks apart, was followed by 18 days of long, dark nights in an ICU room. I sat in the blackness holding Jordyn's hand while she screamed with pain that doctors didn't know how to take away.

Over those 12 months, from one sugar season to the next, I learned that both hope and despair will wax and wane like the seasons themselves when I focus on my circumstances. I learned that joy can be quickly forgotten and only the pain remembered—like mulberry stains that lingered on my fingers long after Mom and Dad enjoyed the pie we baked and left me here, to pack away memories. I decided—in that hard year, from one sugar season to the next—to accept the stains of happy memories that make me weep and the tides of despair that almost crush my spirit. Why? Because of hope. Unwavering, illogical hope.

True hope is solid. Not unlike the foundational beams of my old farmhouse and barn, holding up these old buildings from where they were laid by steady hands centuries ago. Those beams still stand strong, covered in their original bark, their stability obvious to anyone brave enough to venture into the bowels of our dirt-floor cellar.

The foundation of my hope—a hope that is not based on my circumstances—is a God who saves the desperate, the lonely, and the broken while filling voids with his grace.

As I look forward to another winter of sugarmaking here on our little New England homestead, I look forward to the deeply sweet smell that will again linger in our home and the soothing sight of warm auburn jars that will line our counter, but this joy always comes after cold, muddy, messy days. When winter nears an end, the mess is the worst. When I thought my grief had reached the lowest point, I then found myself, already void and empty, beside my daughter in the ICU.

Although I was drained, I was never alone. A strength far beyond my own buoyed me. Truly, the strength of our Creator who has held all things together since the moment he created them enabled me. There's no other explanation, because weak, tired, and in deep mourning for the sudden losses I had already walked through, I had nothing left to offer. I have no idea how I had the strength to go through the rote motions needed to sustain me, let alone query medical experts and learn about a neurological condition that baffled most experts I called around the world. Jordyn was in such depths of pain that she longed for amputation or death. She needed me to be her advocate where there was none. There, in that deep, dark, winter-like place of pain and exhaustion, we called on the Lord together. Empty handed. Deeply troubled. So lost. He met us, he buoyed us, and he brought an emotional spring, so to speak. He provided beauty and hope in that cold, dark place, not unlike the way he provides deliciousness and joy in those snow-covered maples in our cold and windy woods every March.

The following sugaring season, more than a foot of snow still remained in shaded areas on the first day of spring, but daytime temperatures in the 40s left muddy piles in sunny areas of our fields that turned to unassuming ice arenas by evening. As I inspected the treacherous mess that encircled our propane heater and our big pot of sap in our backyard one cold evening, I contemplated how my own life was messy and difficult. Yet God chooses to display his splendor in the maple tree and, yes, in our seasons of hardship.

In fact, call me crazy (it's okay, lots of folks do), but I believe the maple tree is a planting of the Lord; a practical, tasty picture of his provision. Maple syrup? It's a taste of his grace. His creativity. His ingenuity. Sugar from sap. Wow. But, like navigating life, making syrup isn't easy. It's downright difficult.

Yes, my year of loss and pain was messy. I still carry scars, but in the midst of loss and pain God plants glimpses of his splendor. Day by day he's easing despair, and bit by bit he's soothing mourning, replacing despair with praise and mourning with joy. He provided clinical treatments and medical experts who can help my daughter, and he's continually reminding all of our family that his sovereignty and goodness are synonymous and never dependent on circumstances. He alone can bind up the brokenhearted...comfort all who mourn, and provide for those who grieve—to bestow on them . . . the oil of joy instead of mourning, and a garment of praise instead of a spirit of despair. They will be called oaks [or sugar maples] of righteousness, a planting of the Lord for the display of his splendor. (Isaiah 61:1b-3)

Getting to pour delicious, fresh maple syrup on our French toast in the morning is an added bonus. Publishing this, my first book, is part of my healing process. So thank you for the part that you have played. I appreciate that you chose to help sustain a tiny rural farm by purchasing this book, and I hope it provides you with much delight. Seeing the countless mistakes and joys of our labors over the past few years bound up in these pages, helping others avoid mishaps, and encouraging folks to see the blessings of a delicious all-natural sweetener bottled up on their own pantry shelves, well those are truly sweet rewards. I hope the sweetness will spread across pancakes, kitchen pantries, and backyards nationwide. What do you say? Are you in?

Resources

For tree identification, try the apps PlantSnap or PictureThis.

To know the day's perfect temperature to bottle syrup, try the apps SyrupTemp or Sap-TapApps.

The Procter Maple Research Center at the University of Vermont offers numerous, scientific resources at https://www.uvm.edu/~pmrc/.

If you're looking to recycle old sap-collecting tubing, email the Recycling Agricultural Plastics Program at Cornell at agplasticsrecycling@cornell.edu for more information.

Visit us at SoulyRested.com/MapleProducts if you want:

- detailed building instructions of a DIY reverse osmosis system, shown on page 84
- building plans for Bill's DIY tubing reel, described on page 45
- more maple-infused recipes and floral delicacies similar to my lilac syrup
- direct links to the products each professional in this book mentions
- more information about the sugaring equipment, products, and gizmos we love
- links to the small sugar houses that I respect and support (where you can order the most amazing maple products)
- instructions for making a DIY filter press, shown on page 97

Index

About the Author

Michelle Visser is a homesteader in rural New England. She's also a sugarmaker, a fourth-generation gardener, photographer, wife to her high school sweetheart, and mom to four daughters. She likes her sentences loaded with descriptions, sweatshirts always equipped with hoods, and tea black with a sweet chunk of maple sugar. In the Vissers' two-hundred-year-old farmhouse—which sounds more glamorous than it actually is—and on their fourteen rocky, tree-filled acres—which sound smaller than they actually are when you're collecting and carrying gallons of tree sap—the family makes an effort to live life a little more simply. They grow and preserve some of their own food, raise a few farm animals, and make their own all-natural maple sugar.